"*Smart Couples Finish* ... when it comes to mon... and fun to implement. ...

"I know how hard it is to make a personal-finance book user-friendly. Bach has done it. *Smart Couples Finish Rich* picks up where *Smart Women Finish Rich* left off. . . . This is an easy, lively read filled with tips that made me smile and at least once made me laugh."

—*USA Weekend*

"David Bach offers a prescription both to avoid money conflicts and to plan a harmonious future together. Bach's new book offers some valuable new nuggets. The bottom line is action, and Bach's chatty writing style helps motivate you to that end."

—*BusinessWeek*

"*Smart Couples Finish Rich* is a must-read for couples. Bach is a great financial coach . . . he knows how to bring couples together on a topic that often divides them."

—John Gray, author of *Men Are from Mars, Women Are from Venus*

"[David Bach's] advice is heartfelt and worthy. For most couples struggling to make their financial lives smoother, this is a good place to get the dialogue rolling."

—*USA Today*

"My husband and I read this book and found it easy to understand, compassionate, and full of simple financial tools that we could use together. *Smart Couples Finish Rich* takes the guesswork out of the complicated realm of joint finances and leads you down the path of true success."

—Chérie Carter-Scott, author of *If Life Is a Game, These Are the Rules* and *If Success Is a Game, These Are the Rules*

PRAISE FOR *Smart Women Finish Rich*

"David Bach is the one expert to listen to when you're intimidated by your finances. His easy-to-understand program will show you how to afford your dreams."
  —Anthony Robbins, author of *Awaken the Giant Within* and *Unlimited Power*

"*Finally* a book for women that talks about money in a way that makes sense. David Bach is not just an expert in managing money—he's the ultimate motivational coach for women. I can't recommend this book enough. It's a must-read!"
  —Barbara DeAngelis, Ph.D., bestselling author of *Real Moments*

"David Bach both educates and enlightens his readers through his sound investment advice and humor. I highly recommend this book!"
  —Marci Shimoff, coauthor of *Chicken Soup for the Soul*

"[David] Bach gets across some complicated stuff: how to organize a portfolio, keep the taxman at bay, invest in yourself, and earn more, all of which makes this book one of the best overall."
  —*Working Woman*

"Finally, a financial planning guide that addresses the unique issues that women face today. But what I like the most is that David starts with the most important principle: aligning your money with your values."
  —Harry S. Dent, Jr., bestselling author of *The Roaring 2000s*

"Straight-shooting, action-oriented tips for getting a handle on [your] spending and savings habits . . . presented in a straightforward, non-intimidating manner perfect for the personal finance newbie."
  —ABCNews.com

"I love this book! It's more like a motivational seminar than a financial primer. Following David's insightful steps, you will not only increase your net worth, you will change your life. Everyone, not just women, should read this book—at least once!"
  —Barbara Stanny, author of *Prince Charming Isn't Coming*

THE FINISH RICH WORKBOOK

ALSO BY DAVID BACH

Smart Women Finish Rich

Smart Couples Finish Rich

THE
FINISH
RICH

David Bach

WORKBOOK™

Creating a Personalized
Plan for a Richer Future

BROADWAY BOOKS ■ New York

To my incredible parents Bobbi and Marty . . .

you are the best parents and role models a son could ever ask for.

I hope someday to have children and to be the kind of parents you are.

I love you.

BROADWAY

THE FINISH RICH WORKBOOK. Copyright © 2003 by David Bach. All rights reserved. No part of this book may be reproduced or transmitted in any form or by any means, electronic or mechanical, including photocopying, recording, or by any information storage and retrieval system, without written permission from the publisher. For information, address Broadway Books, a division of Random House, Inc., 1745 Broadway, New York, NY 10019.

Broadway Books titles may be purchased for business or promotional use or for special sales. For information, please write to: Special Markets Department, Random House, Inc., 1745 Broadway, New York, NY 10019.

Smart Women Finish Rich, Smart Couples Finish Rich, FinishRich, The Finish Rich Workbook, The FinishRich Book Series, The Automatic Millionaire, Start Young, Finish Rich, FinishRich Seminars, The FinishRich Financial Knowledge Quiz, Purpose-Focused Financial Plan, The FinishRich Inventory Planner, The FinishRich File Folder System, The Latte Factor, The Seven-Day Financial Challenge, The Debt-Free Solution, DOLP, The FinishRich Journal, The FinishRich Advisor Questionnaire, The FinishRich Advisor Gradecard are all trademarks of FinishRich, Inc.

PRINTED IN THE UNITED STATES OF AMERICA

BROADWAY BOOKS and its logo, a letter B bisected on the diagonal, are trademarks of Broadway Books, a division of Random House, Inc.

Visit our Web site at www.broadwaybooks.com

First edition published 2003

Designed by Erin L. Matherne and Tina Thompson

ISBN 0-7679-0481-8

10 9 8 7

CONTENTS

YOUR ROAD MAP TO LIVING—
AND FINISHING—RICH

Welcome to *The Finish Rich Workbook™*. This guidebook for financial planning is designed to help you change your life. In it, you will find a 10-step action plan that will help you create, write down, and move forward toward your personal and financial goals. Whether you are just starting out or are well into your midlife, married or single, this guidebook will make it possible for you to chart a personal road map to a new financial you.

Over the next 238 pages, I'll be your personal financial coach, helping and encouraging you on a journey millions of people much like you have already taken with the help of my books, seminars, PBS show, and personal financial planning practice. As you will discover, this workbook has been specifically devised to speed up the process by introducing you to a series of shortcuts to building wealth and living a life of purpose. With the help of these shortcuts, you'll find your confidence increasing in just a matter of hours (not decades)— to the point where you will be raring to take immediate action toward realizing both your personal and financial dreams.

This workbook can help you IF:

- You are not yet where you want to be financially.
- You've got dreams that are going unfulfilled.
- You're weighed down by credit-card debt.
- You want to protect your family and loved ones.
- You know deep down that you are capable of much more than you are currently doing with your life.
- You want the kind of financial education and proven advice that will enable you to make smart decisions about spending and investing your hard-earned money.
- You want to live a life in line with your values and put the things that matter most to you first.

LEARN IT, WRITE IT, LIVE IT

The Finish Rich Workbook offers you the best ideas from my national bestsellers *Smart Women Finish Rich* and *Smart Couples Finish Rich,* presenting them in a personal journal form that allows you to take action by putting what you want in writing. Over the years I've seen firsthand that the most powerful and effective way of changing your life is (1) to figure out what it is you want, (2) to write it down, and (3) to take action to bring it about. In other words, ***LEARN IT, WRITE IT, LIVE IT.*** When you do the exercises, answer the questions, and fill in the forms you'll find in this workbook, that's just what you will be doing— expressing what you really want out of life, holding it up in front of you, and then positioning yourself to make it happen. In short, you will be harnessing the incredible power of learn it, write it, live it!

This workbook is also meant to make life easier for anyone who regards the world of money and financial planning as boring, complicated, or even impossible to understand. I am here to tell you that it doesn't have to be that way. In fact, as you will see, learning how to manage your finances can be downright simple, even fun.

In addition, this workbook is meant to answer the thousands of e-mails and letters I've received from readers, requesting more details on how to take the techniques I introduced in my FinishRich Book Series™ and put them to work. Specifically, as you read through the pages that follow, you'll quickly learn how to identify your core values, discover your life's purpose, and establish powerful goals that will help you achieve your dreams, both financially and personally. You will also acquire powerfully simple strategies for building lasting wealth and security on just a few dollars a day.

But even if you've never read one of my FinishRich books (*Smart Women Finish Rich* and *Smart Couples Finish Rich)* or taken part in any of our Finish-Rich Seminars™, which are taught throughout North America, this workbook contains everything you need to propel you toward your dreams.

ALL FINANCIAL PROGRESS BEGINS BY TELLING THE TRUTH

Here's a series of million-dollar questions:

- Are you happy right now with where you are financially?
- Are you living the kind of life you want to be living?
- Are your dreams being fulfilled?

These are tough questions—the kind that most people never ask themselves. Most people wish for their dreams but they never actually put together a plan to try to *make* their dreams come true.

Would You Try Something New to Have Greater Happiness, Wealth, or Both?

It's been said that people tend to wind up exactly where they belong in life. That's because we live what we know. Without new knowledge, we can't change. A person is like a fly trying to get out of a house. The little creature can sense the great outdoors on the other side of the windowpane and wants to reach it, and so he crashes into the window over and over again. Because he doesn't know that it's impossible to fly through glass, he keeps trying to get through the windowpane, repeating the exact same action, and achieving the same futile result, until he dies.

Now, to us humans it's obvious how pointless it is for the fly to keep trying the same strategy while hoping for a different result. Yet don't we see people around us every day who keep doing the same things over and over again, even though they don't get the results they want? They date the wrong men or women. They eat too much. They work at jobs they hate. They spend every dime they make so they're stuck living from paycheck to paycheck. And then they wonder: "Why doesn't my life improve? Why can't I get ahead? Why isn't my life more fun?"

Maybe it's because they think of this type of self-defeating, repetitive action not as banging their head against a brick wall (or a solid windowpane) but as being persistent, as not giving up. Maybe you know such a person—perhaps intimately?

CHANGE YOUR ACTIONS, CHANGE YOUR LIFE

The FinishRich system is about becoming just a little bit smarter about what you do and how you do it. Sometimes all it takes to get a great result is a minor change. Think about that fly. How often have you witnessed such a scene and said to yourself, "Hey, fly, just aim four inches lower and you'll be free. Just four inches down, where the window is open, and you'll find a clear path to a whole world outside just waiting for you."

The Window Is Open . . . You Just Need to See It

This workbook can show you where the window is open. But it will be up to you to stop doing what you have been doing and decide instead to aim for the great world of positive change that awaits you. Trust me on this; it's worth the effort. Life is much easier when you aim for the openings.

HOW TO USE THIS WORKBOOK

This workbook is organized into 10 "steps." Ideally, you'll want to read them—and carry them out—in order. That's because they build one on another.

The first few steps are designed to get you ready for action. You will look at your values, goals, and the lessons you've learned in life. You'll write down some ideas about what you want for your future. Then, as you move through the workbook, you'll begin to put your ideas into action. As I said earlier: *Change your action, and you will change your life.*

Whatever you do, don't worry about being "perfect." It's easy to let perfectionism prevent you from taking action. The number-one reason why people fail to make good use of workbooks and written exercises is that they are afraid of not getting it right. Don't be afraid. Your goal with this workbook is not to get every single thing right. Your goal is progress. So if you tend to be a perfectionist, give yourself a break for a few hours and let yourself enjoy the adventure you're about to experience.

The best way to do this is simply to try the exercises. Use a pencil instead of a pen if you're worried that you might want to go back and do them over. When I ask you to stop reading and write something down, remember what those Nike ads say: Just do it. Take the time to think. Let yourself daydream. If you're not in the right frame of mind to do the exercise at that particular moment, then keep reading, but make a specific plan to come back to the exercise later.

If you get stuck on one step, don't feel you have to stop until you get it finished. Keep moving forward, even if you don't finish every single bit of every single exercise. You may find that you don't need to do all 10 steps, or every single one of the exercises. That's okay. It's possible that finishing just one step could change your life. Which step? I don't know. Maybe putting in writing your number-one financial goal for the year will change your life (Introduction). Maybe it will be knowing the truth about yourself and money right now (Step 1), or organizing your finances (Step 2). Maybe you'll begin to see real progress after you get your values down on paper (Step 3). Maybe your life will change when you pinpoint your Latte Factor and take the Seven-Day Financial Challenge (Step 4). Or maybe it will be learning how to get out of debt and retire 10 years early (Step 5), or learning to pay yourself first and create a retirement basket (Step 6), or a security plan (Step 7). Maybe the key for you will be learning how to recapture your dreams (Step 8). Or maybe you really want a financial advisor and you're not sure how to find one (Step 9). Or maybe your big breakthrough will come in Step 10, when you revisit your number-one goal and learn how to overcome any obstacles that seem to stand in your way. Just remember: One idea plus action is the purpose of this workbook.

So, let's begin. Here's a mini-quiz for you to try. Just keep in mind one thing as you write out the answers to the questions below:

All financial progress begins with telling the truth . . .

THE FINISHRICH CLARITY QUESTION

Begin by considering the following question. (Give yourself a few minutes to think it through carefully.)

Over the next year, what one thing would have to happen for you to feel you've made great financial progress?

(For example, you may feel that in order to have made great financial progress by this time next year, you will have to have paid off all your credit-card debt and be saving for a down payment on a house.) Make this message to yourself as specific and measurable as you can. Write your heart out. Share with yourself why this number-one goal for the year is so important to you and how you will feel when you've accomplished it. Most important, write in the past tense—as if you've already achieved the goal. Later in the workbook you will find a place to create more goals for your financial future. For now, simply focus on the single most critical financial goal you have for the next twelve months.

NOW WRITE IT:

★ MY NUMBER-ONE GOAL FOR THE YEAR

Today is _____, 2_____ [write today's date, but a year later].

I have made great financial progress this year by:

_____

_____

_____

_____

_____

_____

_____

_____

_____

_____

_____

_____

_____

_____

_____

_____

_____

_____

_____

_____

_____

YOU, THE MENTOR

No matter what your age, you've probably already learned some important life lessons. With this in mind, imagine yourself as a mentor, sharing your knowledge with someone younger and less experienced. What three things about money have you learned that you want to pass along? It doesn't matter whether your lessons have come from successes or failures. In either case, they can be valuable. So write them down below.

To My Dear Friend:
My Three Most Important Money Lessons Are:
1.
2.
3.

YOUR MONEY-KNOWLEDGE WISH LIST

Now I want you to ask for what you want. What three things do you believe, at a gut level, you need to learn about money? What is your heart telling you right now that you need to know? Write it down.

The Three Things I Need to Learn About Money Are:
1.
2.
3.

YOUR CONFIDENCE FACTOR

The single most important attribute you will need as you progress through this workbook is the confidence to take action. Nothing will ultimately determine your success in life more than this. Without confidence, we simply don't take action to move forward. Without confidence, we often stop just as we're about to act because we don't have the "proof" we need that changing our actions will work. Often, instead of focusing on our strengths, we focus on our weaknesses.

In fact, you already have proof that your actions can lead to success. The trick is to remind yourself of this proof. To do this, I want you to remember your three most important achievements in life. These could be any kinds of successes—personal, career, financial, physical—anything you have done in your life that you are proud of. Think of these as "Atta girl!" or "Atta boy!" experiences. Writing down these successes will give you greater confidence in your life and your ability to take action and overcome challenges. You will instantly feel great simply as a result of recognizing just how strong you are.

So end this step by giving yourself a much-overdue pat on the back. Write down now . . .

The Three Accomplishments I'm Most Proud Of:
1.
2.
3.

CONGRATULATIONS!

Simply by putting these things in writing, you've already made a significant statement to yourself. You've gone beyond just worrying about your finances and have actually begun the process of making your goals concrete—which is the first step to achieving them. You've begun the journey toward living and finishing rich!

Give yourself another pat on the back and turn to Step 1—you're doing great!

FREE! 30 DAYS OF PERSONAL COACHING

As one more way to say thank you for reading this book, I'd like to offer you a new program I've developed. It's called:

The 30-Day FinishRich™ Jumpstart

I created it to keep the readers of my books motivated to take action on their values, goals, and dreams. Please visit my Web site at: www.finishrich.com and sign up today (it's free). And over the next 30 days you'll receive a personal message of financial inspiration. Each message will be short, inspiring, and action oriented. Enjoy!

START THE JOURNEY TO LIVING AND FINISHING RICH: *KNOW WHERE YOU COME FROM*

You're beginning an exciting journey. What's most exciting about it is that *you* are in the driver's seat. When you decide to live rich, you're on your way to having the kind of life you want. Getting there begins right here. In Step 1, you're going to put your intelligence, life experiences, and courage to good use by taking a quick and powerful look at yourself and your finances. I'm going to help you think through what's working in your life and what's not. Then we'll discover what you know—and don't know—about your finances. The goal of this first step is to get you revved up and ready to take action. Today is the day you take control of your financial future. As I said in the Introduction, you're going to **LEARN IT, WRITE IT, LIVE IT!**

As we go through this workbook together, I hope you'll think of me as your personal financial coach. Imagine that we are in your car heading toward your ideal destination: a rich and rewarding future. You're doing the driving and I'm in the passenger seat, guiding you and rooting for you as you discover new truths that bring you closer to your financial goals and dreams. Together we'll get you to where you want to be.

A QUICK TRUTH TEST: WHAT IS WORKING FOR YOU?

When it comes to money . . .
there are things that work and things that don't work.

I'm sure you already suspect that there's room for improvement in some aspects of your financial life. That's why you picked up this workbook in the first place. In my experience, there are always some things in life that work and others that don't. This is especially true when it comes to your money. Sure, it's nice to know what parts of your financial program are already on track. (You may discover you're in better shape than you think you are!) But it's even more important to acknowledge what is not working financially so you can strive to improve it. After all, until you know what's broken, how can you figure out how to fix it?

The most important piece of advice I can give you as you take the following quiz is to be absolutely honest with yourself. If you don't like your answers, that's okay. It's important to know the truth. The crucial information you'll get from this simple exercise will free you to take action and make positive changes for your future.

Take a moment to assess the following areas of your financial life. You may not know *why* each area is working or not, but chances are you have a sense of *whether* it is. So for each of the phrases below, simply check the appropriate ending: "working" or "not working."

WHAT'S WORKING FOR YOU?	Working	Not Working
My finances are	_____	_____
My knowledge about money is	_____	_____
My relationship with money is	_____	_____
My relationship with my significant other and money is	_____	_____
My ability to save is	_____	_____
My ability to control spending is	_____	_____
My control of credit-card spending is	_____	_____
My credit record is	_____	_____
My savings are	_____	_____
My career is	_____	_____
My retirement account is	_____	_____
My investment accounts are	_____	_____
My will or trust is	_____	_____
My life insurance is	_____	_____
My health insurance is	_____	_____
My checking account is	_____	_____
My financial file system at home is	_____	_____

Look over your answers. What do you see? On balance, is your financial situation working or not working? If you are like most people, you probably have more check marks in the "not working" column than in the "working" column. After you finish this workbook, you should take this quiz again. You'll be amazed by the incredible progress you will have made.

WHO TAUGHT YOU ABOUT MONEY?

Let me ask you a question: While you were growing up, did you have a good financial role model? Did one or both of your parents coach you about money? Did they talk to you about it at the dinner table, or comment constructively when the mistakes or successes of others came up for discussion? Or was money a taboo subject? In most families, money is never talked about. Many parents will discuss sex with their kids before they will tell them how much they earn. Think back. What happened at your house? Your parents may never have given you a money lesson, but you certainly learned by watching them. I want you to write out the three most important lessons you learned from your parents about money. Keep in mind that these lessons may or may not be positive ones. Doing this exercise may tell you a lot about how you relate to money now.

From My Parents, I Learned the Following Three Things About Money:
1.
2.
3.

Interesting, isn't it? The first time I did this exercise, I was surprised at what I wrote down. One of the first things that came to me was "Money is meant to be spent and enjoyed." My parents started with literally nothing, and as they began to have financial success, they enjoyed it. Yet they also watched their spending. My mom clipped coupons every weekend, and together we would use them when we shopped at the grocery store. I hated this at the time, because it took forever to get the shopping done. But my mom was always proud of how much we saved. The lesson I learned from this is that you can balance enjoying your money with saving it.

Again, it's important to remember that we sometimes learn money lessons from our parents that are negative. If that is your situation, take heart. As soon as you recognize that what they taught you isn't working, you can put it behind you. The future of what you learn belongs to you. That's what this workbook is all about.

YOUR MONEY VALUES

As a financial advisor, I specialize in creating what we call a Purpose-Focused Financial Plan™. What this means is that I want to help you discover what your true values about money actually are. Once you know this, you can focus your time and energy on what matters most to you. You'll find that instead of having to "motivate yourself" to make financial changes, you'll be pulled in the right direction by the power of your values.

Let's get started by thinking in general terms about your money values. (Later on, in Step 3, we will take an in-depth look at your top personal values regarding life and money, and create what I call a Value Circle™.) For the moment, I want you simply to write down what money means to you. To do this, finish the sentence "Money is . . ."

For example:

Money Is . . .
1.   POWER
2.   HAPPINESS
3.   GREED
4.   BAD
5.   GOOD

Notice that these answers are all descriptive words that have to do with what money *means*. Now it's your turn. Record today's date above the first column, then finish the sentence "Money is" by filling in the 10 blanks on the next page. Write your answers quickly so that you don't overthink them. You want to record your "gut responses."

Money Is . . .
Date: _____
1.
2.
3.
4.
5.
6.
7.
8.
9.
10.

What did you just learn? Again, you may like what you wrote down, or you may be surprised by your responses. After you've finished this entire workbook, I want you to come back to this section and do this exercise again. Cover up your answers from today and then fill in the blanks on the next page. Aim to do this exactly 30 days from today. I think you'll be surprised by how much your thinking has changed and how far you've come in a short period of time.

Money Is . . .
Date: _____
1.
2.
3.
4.
5.
6.
7.
8.
9.
10.

Now let's take a look at how much you know about your own financial situation.

THE FINISHRICH™ FINANCIAL KNOWLEDGE QUIZ

You now have a better idea of what money means to you personally. That's a good start. But if you're going to improve your financial profile, you also need to know *what you know* about your finances—that is, what you're doing with the money and resources you have. After all, before you can start planning how to get more out of your money and how to invest it wisely, you need to know exactly how much you've got, where it's currently parked, and just how accessible it is.

Even if you share your finances with a life partner, take this simple true/false quiz alone. You need to know how accurately (or inaccurately) *you* understand your current financial situation. Many readers of the FinishRich books have reported that this quiz was the driving force that finally got them to take action and improve their finances. Take it now for yourself and see what you learn:

T ❑ F ❑   I know my current net worth (that is, the current value of the assets I have minus the liabilities I owe).

T ❑ F ❑   I have a solid grasp of what my fixed monthly overhead is, including property taxes and all forms of insurance.

T ❑ F ❑   I know how much life insurance I carry. I know exactly what the death benefits are, how much cash value there is in the policy (if any), and what rate the money is earning (if applicable).

T ❑ F ❑   I have reviewed my life insurance policy sometime in the last 12 to 24 months and am comfortable that I am paying a competitive rate in today's insurance market.

T ❑ F ❑   I know the current value of my home, the size of my mortgage, the interest rate on the mortgage, and how much equity I have in my home. I also know the length of my mortgage-payment schedule and how much it would cost per month to pay down the mortgage in half the time.

OR

T ❑ F ❑   I know how much rent I pay, when my lease expires, how much of a security deposit I gave the landlord, and what renewal rights I have.

T ❑ F ❑   I know what type of homeowner's or renter's insurance I have and what the deductibles are. I know whether or not my policy would provide me with "today's replacement cost," or actual cash value, if my home and/or property were destroyed or stolen.

T ❑ F ❑   I know the nature and size of all of my investments, including cash, checking accounts, savings accounts, money market accounts, CDs, Treasury bills, savings bonds, mutual funds, annuities, stocks and bonds, real estate investments, and collectibles such as stamps, coins, artwork, etc. I also know where all the relevant paperwork is kept.

T ❑ F ❑   I know the annualized returns of all the above-mentioned investments.

T ❑ F ❑   I know the current value of all of my retirement accounts, including 401(k) plans, 403(b) plans, IRAs, Roth IRAs, SEP-IRAs, Keogh plans, company pension plans, etc. I know where the statements for these accounts are kept and I have a solid grasp of how all my accounts performed last year.

T ❑ F ❑   I know what percentage of my income (or the total with my partner) I am saving.

T ❑ F ❑   I know how much I am putting into my retirement account, whether that amounts to the maximum allowable contribution, whether my employer is making matching contributions, and what my vesting schedule is.

T ❑ F ❑   I know how much money I will be getting from Social Security when I retire, and what my pension benefits (if any) will be.

T ❑ F ❑   I know whether or not I have a living will or living trust, what its provisions are, and how up-to-date it is.

T ❏ F ❏ I know whether my income would be protected by disability insurance should I (or my partner) become unable to work. If I do have disability insurance, I know the amount of the coverage, when the benefits would start, and whether they would be taxable. If I don't have disability insurance, I know why I don't.

T ❏ F ❏ (If applicable) I know what my partner's wishes are regarding medical treatment (including being kept alive by artificial means) in the event he/she falls seriously ill or is seriously injured. I know whether or not our will includes a valid power of attorney covering such situations. I also know how my partner feels about being an organ donor.

T ❏ F ❏ I have a financial advisor and I like him/her. He/she is a true partner in my financial growth. I've also done my due diligence on his/her credentials and checked out his/her background on the NASD Web site, www.nasd.com.

T ❏ F ❏ I'm comfortable with my knowledge of the Economic Growth and Tax Relief Reconciliation Act of 2001. I know that there were more than 400 new tax regulations created by this law, and I'm using some of them to save more money and legally pay less in taxes.

I completed this quiz on (date) _____.

SCORING:

Give yourself one point for every time you answered "True," and zero for every time you answered "False."

16 to 20 points. Great job! You obviously have a good grasp of the state of your finances.

9 to 13 points. You're not completely in the dark, but your knowledge is inadequate in some important areas.

Under 8 points. Your chances of being hurt financially because of inadequate knowledge are enormous. You need to learn how to protect yourself against future financial disaster.

If you scored well on this test, congratulations! But don't stop to celebrate now. Even the world's leading money experts constantly seek out new knowledge, and you should, too. If you didn't do as well as you would have liked, don't worry. I promise that the remaining steps in this workbook are designed to give you the tools to pass this quiz later with flying colors. As with the other exercises, make sure you date the quiz and take it again after you've completed the workbook. By doing this, you'll be able to see in black and white the massive progress you've made, both financially and personally.

FINANCIAL CLARITY IS POWER

You've just taken a quick, meaningful look at your feelings, values, and knowledge about money. You've learned what you know and what you don't know about your financial situation. Your new knowledge is power—it will be a big help to you as you continue with Step 2 and the journey ahead.

Next, we are going to begin the process of figuring out where your money is. Keep going. You're doing great!

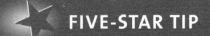

FIVE-STAR TIP

If you are married or have a significant other in your life, I suggest you try and get him/her to go through this workbook with you. A great way to raise the subject of doing this together is to ask your partner to take the FinishRich Knowledge Quiz. Make a photocopy of it and give it to him/her (you have my permission to reproduce it for personal use). See what his/her response is and how he/she scores.

You may be surprised to find that your partner is more motivated to work with you on your money "stuff" than you thought. You may also find out that you know more about the family's finances than your partner. While this may feel good, it is, in fact, *not* good. It is critical to your family's long-term financial health that you both be equally knowledgeable about money.

For more information on how to plan your life financially as a couple, visit our Web site at www.finishrich.com. (I've posted an excerpt from my book *Smart Couples Finish Rich* that you can read for free.)

FIND YOUR MONEY:
DISCOVER YOUR NET WORTH

DO YOU KNOW WHERE YOUR MONEY IS?

In Step 1, you took the first important step toward planning your financial future. You've begun to understand what wealth means to you. Now it's time to find your money.

If I asked you about your current financial status, could you—right now—write down a list of all your assets and liabilities, including your investments, bank accounts, mortgages, and credit-card debts? Do you have an organized filing system in which all of your financial documents can be found easily? Or have you told yourself, "Someday I'll get my financial stuff organized at home," only to find that "someday" never comes?

In Step 2, we're going to make sure you know exactly where your money is. Think back to the FinishRich Financial Knowledge Quiz in Step 1. If you didn't score as well as you would have liked, that's okay; we are about to start fixing the problems you discovered as a result of taking the quiz.

Knowing Where Your Money Is Sounds Obvious, but Trust Me—Most People Don't Have a Clue

Getting your finances organized is one of the most powerful keys to financial security. Why? Because until you know exactly where you stand, it's impossible to plan where you want to go. Until you know what your assets are and where you spend your money, you simply cannot make a financial plan that is based on reality. You've got to have a starting point, and that starting point depends on getting your financial documents in one place. Here's the good news: Over the years, I've

FIVE-STAR TIP

If you're not reading this at home, go ahead and finish this section of the workbook. Then take out your calendar and make a date to do this exercise when you are home. I can't tell you how important it is that you commit to creating your own FinishRich File Folder System. I receive more grateful e-mail from FinishRich readers about this exercise than any other. In fact, I've heard from hundreds of people that doing this simple exercise was the catalyst that motivated them to take action in other areas of their financial lives. Remember, the only way this workbook is going to change your financial life is if you're willing to take action. So set a date and don't cancel it!

I will organize my financial folders no later than [insert date] _____.

created a system that helps people get organized quickly and easily. The system is so simple, in fact, that you will probably be able to get all of your personal financial information in order in less than an hour. Do this step in exactly the order it's laid out, and you'll have a new financial foundation built by the end of the day.

THE FINISHRICH FILE FOLDER SYSTEM™

This is your first job—to find your stuff! Here's what to do: First, get yourself a dozen or so hanging folders and a box of at least 50 file folders to put inside them. Then label the folders as follows:

1. ❑ Label the first one **"Tax Returns."**
In it, put eight file folders, one for each of the last seven years plus one for this year. Mark the year on each folder's tab and put into it all of that year's important tax documents, such as W-2 forms, 1099s, and (most important) a copy of all the tax returns you filed for that year. Hopefully, you've at least saved your old tax returns. If you haven't but used a professional tax preparer in the past, call him or her and ask for back copies. As a rule, you should keep old tax records for at least seven years in case the IRS wants to audit you. I recommend hanging on to them even longer, but that's up to you.

2. ❏ Label the second hanging folder "**Retirement Accounts**."
This is where you're going to keep all of your retirement-account statements. You should create a file for each retirement account that you and your partner have. If the two of you have three IRAs and a 401(k) plan, then you should have a separate file for each. And don't forget to write whose IRA it is on the top of each file. The most important thing to keep in these folders are the quarterly statements. You *don't* need to keep the prospectuses that the mutual-fund companies mail you each quarter. However, if you have a company retirement account, you should definitely keep the sign-up package because it tells you what investment options you have—something you should review annually.

3. ❏ Label the third hanging folder **"Social Security."**
You should put your most recent Social Security Benefits Statement in this folder. If you didn't receive one in the mail, go online to www.ssa.gov to request one. If you don't have Internet access, you can telephone the Social Security Administration toll-free at 800-772-1213.

4. ❏ Label the fourth hanging folder "**Investment Accounts**."
In this folder you put files for each investment account you have that is not a retirement account. If you own mutual funds, maintain a brokerage account, or own individual stocks, each and every statement you receive that is related to these investments should go in a particular folder. If you have a spouse or partner and the two of you have both individual and joint accounts, create separate files for them as well.

5. ❏ Label the fifth hanging folder **"Savings and Checking Accounts."**
If you have a spouse or partner and the two of you have separate checking and savings accounts, create separate file folders for them. Keep your monthly bank statements here.

6. ❏ Label the sixth hanging folder **"Household Accounts."**
If you own your own home, this one should contain the following file folders:
- "House Title," into which you put all your title information, such as title reports and title insurance policies (if you can't find this stuff, call your real estate agent or title company)

- "Home Improvements," where you should keep all your receipts for any home-improvement work you do (since home-improvement expenses can be added to the cost basis of your house when you sell it, you should keep these receipts for as long as you own your house)
- "Home Mortgage," for all your mortgage statements (which you should check regularly, since mortgage companies often *don't credit you properly*). If you're a renter, this folder should contain your lease, the receipt for your security deposit, and the receipts or canceled checks for your rental payments.

7. ❏ Label the seventh hanging folder **"Credit-Card DEBT."**
Make sure you capitalize the word "DEBT" so it stands out and bothers you every time you see it. I'm not kidding. I'll explain later how to deal with credit-card debt. For the time being, my hope is that this won't be one of your larger hanging folders. You should create a separate file folder for each credit-card account you have. For many people, this folder may contain more than a dozen files. I've actually met some with as many as 30. However many files you have, keep all your monthly statements in them. And hang on to them. Because I itemize my tax deductions, I keep all my credit-card records for at least seven years in case the IRS ever decides to audit me.

8. ❏ Label the eighth hanging folder **"Other Liabilities."**
In here go all of your records dealing with debts other than your mortgage and your credit-card accounts. These would include college loans, car loans, personal loans, etc. Each debt should have its own file folder, which should contain the loan note and your payment records.

9. ❏ Label the ninth hanging folder **"Insurance."**
It will contain separate file folders for each of your insurance policies, including health, life, car, homeowner's or renter's, disability, long-term care, etc. In these folders put the appropriate policy and all the related payment records. If your insurance is provided by an employer, include all the brochures and other informational material you've received about your coverage.

10. ❑ Label the tenth hanging folder **"Family Will or Trust."**
This should have a copy of your most recent will or living trust, along with the business card of the attorney who set it up.

11. ❑ If you have children, put together a folder labeled **"Children's Accounts."**
It should hold all statements and other records pertaining to college savings accounts or other investments that you have made for your kids.

12. ❑ Create a folder called **"FinishRich Inventory Planner™."**
This is where you're going to put the worksheet beginning on page 190 of this workbook after you've filled it out. This folder will also contain a file in which you keep a running semiannual total of your net worth—a vital record that will help you keep track of your financial progress.

13. ❑ Label the thirteenth folder **"Where Does the Money Go?"**
In it, store the "Where Does Your Money Really Go?" worksheet found on page 19. This critical form will show you in black and white where you are spending your money. For some of you this may be the most important folder you create.

That's it. You're done. Thirteen files—twelve if you don't have children. Not so tough, right?

As you complete this assignment, you may notice that some folders are empty because they're not applicable to your financial situation. Keep those folders anyway. They may pertain to you at some point in the future after you've created your financial plan.

You may also have discovered that you're missing a few documents. In some cases, this may be because you never received or created the document in the first place; in others, you may have inadvertently thrown them out. That's okay. Simply use the space below to make a note of what you don't have and whom you need to contact to fill in the gaps. Commit yourself to hunting down those missing pieces of your financial picture within the next 48 hours. When you have obtained a document, check it off under "Acquired."

	Missing Information	Source	Acquired (✓)
1.			
2.			
3.			
4.			
5.			
6.			
7.			

You now have an orderly place for all of your current and future financial documents. As a result of completing this simple assignment, everything else you do from here on out will be much easier. In just a few hours, I bet you've gotten your finances more organized than they've been in years.

IT'S OKAY TO THROW AWAY OUTDATED STUFF

Do you still have a huge pile of papers that don't seem to fit in any of your folders? You can probably get rid of most of it. The reason I made the FinishRich File Folder System so specific is that many of us keep too much information. You don't need to keep everything—especially if it's outdated. Here's a list of items you should consider throwing away:

- Outdated warranties
- Outdated instruction manuals
- Outdated wills or trusts (provided you've created a new one)
- Outdated health insurance policies
- Credit-card statements for closed tax years (a closed tax year is usually considered to be three years old—at most, keep statements for seven years)

- Old annual reports from stocks and/or mutual funds
- Canceled checks for closed tax years (again, keep for seven years at most)
- Old brokerage statements more than seven years old (unless they have cost-basis information you feel you need)
- Old reading materials (if you have clipped articles that are older than 30 days, toss them; you're never going to read them and they're probably outdated anyway)
- Old investment newsletters (some people keep these things for years because they paid for them—let them go)

FIVE-STAR TIP

A Secret for Couples

If you are a part of a couple, this is a great assignment to do together. But I'm also a realist. It's possible that you are more motivated to do this exercise than your partner. If this describes your situation, my advice is to try to set up a "clean out the money files" date. If you ask your partner nicely and share your enthusiasm for the project, you may inspire him or her to join you. If you strike out, go ahead and do it yourself. My experience is that once your partner sees you with your files spread out (especially if you do it out in the open at the kitchen table or in the living room), he or she will come around and want to get involved.

WHERE DOES YOUR MONEY REALLY GO?

You're getting organized, which is great. But you probably still couldn't tell me exactly where your money goes. One of the most important parts of getting your financial life together is having a solid grasp of exactly what your current cash flow is. By filling out the form below, you'll discover where you are spending your money. Doing this exercise requires only pen and paper, and maybe a calculator. It's simple, yet powerful. Later, if you want to use a computer software program to track your spending, go for it. Two of the programs I like best are Quicken (available at www.quicken.com) and Microsoft Money (www.microsoft.com/money). I'll tell you more about them later.

WHERE DOES YOUR MONEY REALLY GO?	
First, determine how much you earn.	
Your Income	
Wages, salary, tips, commissions, self-employment income	$ _____
Dividends from stocks, bonds, mutual funds, savings accounts, CDs, etc.	$ _____
Income from rental property	$ _____
Income from trust accounts (usually death benefits from an estate)	$ _____
Alimony, child support, widow's benefits	$ _____
Social Security benefits	$ _____
Other income	$ _____
TOTAL MONTHLY INCOME	$ _____

WHERE DOES YOUR MONEY REALLY GO?

Second, determine what you spend monthly.

Your Expenses

Taxes

Federal income taxes	$ _____
State income taxes	$ _____
FICA (Social Security Taxes)	$ _____
Property taxes	$ _____
TOTAL TAXES	$ _____

Housing

Mortgage payments or rent on primary residence	$ _____
Mortgage payment on rental or income property	$ _____
Utilities	$ _____
Homeowner's or renter's insurance	$ _____
Repairs or home maintenance	$ _____
Cleaning service	$ _____
Television cable	$ _____
Home phone	$ _____
Landscaping and pool service	$ _____
Monthly Internet service	$ _____
Condo or association dues	$ _____
TOTAL HOUSING	$ _____

Auto

Car loan or lease	$ _____
Gas	$ _____
Car insurance	$ _____
Car phone	$ _____
Repairs or service	$ _____
Parking	$ _____
Bridge tolls	$ _____
TOTAL AUTO	$ _____

WHERE DOES YOUR MONEY REALLY GO?

Insurance

Life insurance	$ _____
Disability insurance	$ _____
Long-term care insurance	$ _____
Liability insurance (umbrella policy)	$ _____
TOTAL INSURANCE	$ _____

Food

Groceries	$ _____
Food outside of home	$ _____
TOTAL FOOD	$ _____

Personal Care

Clothing	$ _____
Cleaning/dry cleaning	$ _____
Cosmetics	$ _____
Health club dues and/or personal trainer	$ _____
Entertainment	$ _____
Country club dues	$ _____
Association memberships	$ _____
Vacations	$ _____
Hobbies	$ _____
Education	$ _____
Magazines	$ _____
Gifts	$ _____
TOTAL PERSONAL CARE	$ _____

Medical

Health care insurance	$ _____
Dental insurance	$ _____
Prescription and monthly medicines	$ _____
Chiropractic/therapist/etc.	$ _____
Doctor or dentist expenses (copayments)	$ _____
TOTAL MEDICAL	$ _____

WHERE DOES YOUR MONEY REALLY GO?

Children

Child support	$ _____
Babysitter/child care	$ _____
School tuition	$ _____
School activities (sports, drama, art, band, etc.)	$ _____
Clothing	$ _____
Tutoring	$ _____
College funding	$ _____
TOTAL CHILDREN	$ _____

Miscellaneous

Credit-card expenses	$ _____
Loan payments	$ _____
Anything you can think of that I missed!	$ _____
TOTAL MISCELLANEOUS EXPENSES	$ _____

TOTAL MONTHLY EXPENSES	$ _____
Murphy's Law Factor	
Take the total expenses and increase by 10 percent	$ _____
TOTAL MONTHLY INCOME (from page 19)	
Minus **total monthly expenses** (after Murphy's Law)	$ _____
NET CASH FLOW (AVAILABLE FOR SAVINGS OR INVESTMENTS)	$ _____

Now that you can see where your money winds up, how do you feel? Are you surprised? Don't panic if your net cash flow isn't what you'd hoped. Just by doing this exercise you've put yourself on the right track. Knowing the truth is the all-important first step. Now we can work together to improve your finances. In Step 4, I'll show you how to get your spending under control and improve your bottom line. Meanwhile, let's finish getting organized so that the road ahead on your financial journey will be as smooth as possible.

FIVE-STAR TIP

If you would prefer to skip the math and have your expenses calculated for you, visit www.finishrich.com. In the resource center, go to the section called "Getting Your Finances Organized" and click onto the "Where Does the Money Go?" worksheet. There you can use an online tool that will help you figure your monthly expenses quickly and automatically.

IF YOU REALLY WANT TO SIMPLIFY YOUR LIFE, DO WHAT I DID

Here's the truth: Paying your bills and keeping track of your expenses, net worth, and assets can be a pain in the butt. I personally hate these "house-keeping" chores. Fortunately, I've found ways to make them less tedious. What follows is my tried-and-true advice on how to handle these important—but annoying—financial tasks. I guarantee these suggestions will make your life significantly easier.

> **SUGGESTION NO. 1**
> **Pay Your Bills Online**

I pay all my bills—both personal and business—online. Specifically, I use what is called an "online bill presentment company." What this means is that rather than showing up in my mailbox, my bills are sent directly to the presentment company. When they arrive, the company notifies me by e-mail and posts them on a secure Web site. I can then go online and pay them with a click of my mouse. It literally takes me five minutes a month to pay my personal bills and maybe 10 minutes a month to pay my corporate bills. This same process used to take me five to 10 hours a month when I did things the old-fashioned way—by writing checks. I've been using this system for two years now and here's why I love it:

- Once it's set up, it's a breeze to use and saves time.
- I don't receive bills at home, so I don't have to open them and organize them every day. There are no change-of-address worries. (When Michelle and I moved from San Francisco to New York, we didn't have to worry about any bills going astray. Everything stayed the same because all our bills continued to go to the presentment company.)

- I can order a CD-ROM disk each year with a record of all our bills and transactions for the year.
- After I pay my bills, the information can be automatically downloaded into Quicken or some other money-management software system. This saves hours of entering the information manually.
- Because I use a third-party company, I'm not tied to any particular financial institution, such as a bank. If I paid my bills online through my bank and then wanted to change banks, I would have to redirect every single bill (a huge hassle). By using a third-party company, if I ever change banks, all I need to do is click a few buttons (to provide the bill presentment company with my new bank account information) and the money will instantly be taken out of my new account. Very convenient.

Here are the best three online bill payment companies I know:

1. www.statusfactory.com

2. www.quickenbillpay.com

3. www.paytrust.com

Check out all three and see what you think. Most of these companies charge fees starting at about $9 a month. The price usually depends on how many checks you write.

SUGGESTION NO. 2
Download All Your Expenses into a Financial Software Program

My wife and I currently use Quicken for our personal finances and Quickbooks (www.quicken.com) for our business. Friends who use Microsoft Money (www.microsoft.com) tell me this software is just as good (some swear it is better). Whatever your personal preference, I recommend you find one you like and use it regularly. In our house, my wife Michelle and I download all our credit-card expenses from the bill-payment company into our Quicken software every month. This gives us a nearly complete breakdown of exactly where our money is going. (The only aspect of our spending that we can't track automatically is our cash outlays.) As a result, our family record-keeping has really improved and we can track our business expenses down to the last penny.

FIVE-STAR TIP

The secret to getting the most out of financial software like Quicken or Microsoft Money is automation. My experience is that people who try to do everything manually don't stick with it. After all, if you have to enter every expense by hand, it can take hours. That's why I recommend using online bill-paying and bank account services that allow you to download information directly into your financial software.

SUGGESTION NO. 3
Track Your Investments Online

I can't imagine not being able to track my investments online. I log on to my computer and check my accounts weekly, if not daily. In this way, it takes only a few minutes to get a crystal-clear picture of my finances. Most banks and brokerage firms today offer online access to accounts, yet many people still don't take advantage of it. If you have investments and you don't have this kind of online access, call your bank or brokerage firm today to get a password that will enable you to review your account information from your home computer. Doing this will simplify your life—and put an up-to-the-minute snapshot of your financial situation at your fingertips.

FIVE-STAR TIP

Another reason to check your accounts online is to protect yourself from fraud. Not long ago, a broker in Ohio was arrested for allegedly swindling tens of millions of dollars from his clients by "doctoring" their statements. The broker was caught after some of his clients went online and noticed that their account values didn't match the information on the statements he'd been sending them. (One woman who thought she had $2.5 million in assets discovered that her account was actually worth only $100,000.) The only downside to getting online access to your investment account is the risk that a hacker might gain access to your personal financial information through the Internet. So make sure to find out about your bank or brokerage's online security policies. You might also consider getting firewall software for your computer at home.

You Don't Have to Be a Tech Geek or Computer Guru to Do Any of This

If you think my advice is too high-tech for you, relax. My computer skills are really basic. I don't even like to read instructions. If a program isn't super easy, I won't use it. The three timesaving suggestions I described above are just that—super easy. You can set up the computer software and online accounts in no time. Once that's done, you'll be able to manage your money in just minutes a month. Trust me, it's worth the few hours it will take you. You'll probably wind up saving an entire day of your time every month. To me, that's like gaining an extra Saturday each month to do what you want. That's almost two weeks a year that you've freed up to spend with your family or on your hobbies. That's worth it.

CONGRATULATIONS!

You did it. You've done more in this step to organize your money than most people do in their entire lives.

You're making huge progress, so let's keep going. In Step 3, we'll create a financial plan based on your most deeply held values.

CREATE YOUR PURPOSE-FOCUSED FINANCIAL PLAN™

WHAT ARE YOUR VALUES?

Does this question surprise you? You may well wonder why we bring up values when the subject is supposed to be money. Isn't the aim of this workbook to help you to figure out how much money you have now, how much you need to finish rich, and how to get from here to there?

Of course it is. But while it's absolutely critical to know what you have in dollars and cents, it's equally essential to understand what it will take to create a rich life for you as an individual. And a rich life isn't defined by bank balances alone. It comes from focusing on *what matters most to you*. What do you care most deeply about? What do you stand for? The answers to these questions depend mainly on your values.

Your Life Values Should Determine Every Life Decision You Make

Think about it: What you value affects every aspect of your life—where you live, how much you spend, what you focus your time and energy on. Your values color your communications with your partner, family, and friends. They influence how you raise your children. They dictate how you feel about what you have in life. Your values also determine how hard you are willing to work to achieve your financial goals and how much money you'll actually need at retirement.

As a financial planner, I specialize in doing what we call Purpose-Focused Financial Planning™. What this means is that before we can figure out how much money you'll need for your future, we need a clear idea of what you see as your purpose in life.

This concept often surprises people. The investment industry has gotten all of us so focused on what it calls "retirement planning" that everyone thinks personal finance is all about determining how much money you need at retirement. But how can I help you figure out how much money you'll need until we know what kind of life you hope to lead?

What's the Purpose of Money in Your Life?

As a financial planner, I've learned that when all is said and done, money is good for three basic things in life. It helps people:

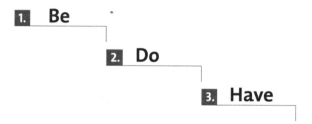

1. Be

2. Do

3. Have

Let me explain what I mean by this.

First of all, money allows people to live in a way that defines who they are (Be). Second, money makes it possible for people to take the actions that will lead to the kind of lives they think they want (Do). Third, money enables people to buy stuff (Have).

Ideally, the lives we lead, the actions we take, and the stuff we buy all line up with our values. In my experience, though, too many people start by focusing on "having," then turn to "doing," and may or may not ever get around to the "being" part of the equation. In other words, they go about their financial lives backwards. They spend so much time on "having" and "doing" that they never take a moment to make sure that who they are is who they want to be.

A Purpose-Focused Financial Plan puts first things first, so that you plan your finances around what matters most *to you*. With this in mind, let's get your priorities down on paper by creating a Value Circle™.

FIVE-STAR TIP

Don't Skip This Step

Some of you may think that these value exercises are a waste of time, that they are nothing more than New Age, feel-good fluff. Well, there is nothing New Age about looking at your values. The Greek philosopher Socrates was talking about this exact type of thing back in 400 B.C. The key to human advancement, he taught, could be expressed in two powerful words: "Know thyself."

Don't be tempted to skip this step and move on to the next one. If you need another reason to examine your values, here's one: consumerism. It's a trap that the best of us fall into. We live in a society in which we are bombarded with more than 3,000 marketing messages a day—every one of them designed to separate us from our money by convincing us we need more stuff. Only in America do people have so many possessions that they don't have room to park their cars in their garages. So what do we do? We go to a storage facility and rent a space to store our things, which may not even be paid for yet because we still have those enormous credit-card bills. Then we go to work every day (often at jobs we don't like) to pay for everything. We work so hard that we never get to step back and look at our lives or ask ourselves: "Do I like who I am?" "Am I being who I want to be?"

Knowing your values can help you stop this vicious cycle. When you understand what's important to you, it becomes much easier to focus on who you want to *be,* then on what you want to *do,* and, finally, on what "stuff" you *really* want to have. Trust me, the Value Circle exercise can change your life.

THE VALUE CIRCLE™

Let's get started. Imagine that you are arriving at the offices of FinishRich, Inc. You're going to meet with me in order to create your own personal Value Circle. On the desk in front of you is a blank Value Circle sheet (found on page 31), waiting for you to tell yourself—and me—what matters most to you.

Here are some simple tips to get you through the process:

1. **Relax.** This is not a test. It's meant to be fun. The objective here is simple honesty. Write down only what feels right at a gut level. Don't list a value just because you think it "looks" good. If it doesn't reflect how you feel in your gut, it won't really mean anything to you, and you won't focus or act on it.

2. **Start with the simple question,** What is really important to you? When you think about your life and things that really matter, what value is most important to you? What's the purpose of money in your life?

3. **Remember to stay focused on values**—not goals, not things, not stuff to do or buy. If, say, you worry a lot about money, you might be tempted to list as a value "having a million dollars." But that's not a value; it's a goal. The underlying value in this case would probably be security or freedom. The million dollars is just a way to fulfill one of those values. Similarly, many people say they want to travel. But "travel" is not a value; it's a thing to do. The value that travel promotes might be fun, excitement, or personal growth. See the chart on page 32. It demonstrates the difference between a value and a goal.

4. **As they occur to you,** write down values in the Value Circle until you have listed five core values that you can commit to focusing on over the next 12 months. You might find out that there are more than five values that you want to focus on. Some of my clients and students have come up with as many as 10 values. There's nothing wrong with that, if you are serious about your commitment. It's just that in my experience most people find it difficult to focus on more than five at a time.

5. That's it. You have completed the Value Circle. Give yourself a pat on the back.

EXAMPLE: KIM'S VALUE CIRCLE ™

YOUR TURN: YOUR OWN VALUE CIRCLE ™

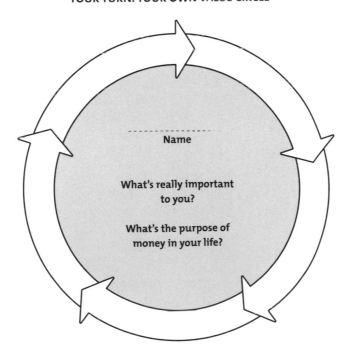

YOUR OWN VALUE CIRCLE™

If You Find Yourself Getting Stuck . . .

If you find yourself getting stuck . . . again, don't try not to overthink this exercise. Start by writing down whatever seems important. You can refine your answers as you go along.

Some of you may be struggling with the difference between a value and a goal. Remember that values are about being; they define a way of life. Goals tend to be about having and doing; they usually involve stuff. To help you differentiate between the two, I've listed below some common values and some common goals. Use these examples to help you get started if you are having trouble, but don't just copy them down. In order for this exercise to work, you really have to care—at a gut level—about the values you choose.

VALUES VS. GOALS	
VALUES	**GOALS**
Security	Retire with a million dollars
Freedom	Pay off mortgage
Happiness	Be debt free
Peace of mind	Not worry about debt
Fun	Travel
Excitement	Ski with friends
Power	Be the boss
Family	Spend more time with kids
Marriage	Plan more "date nights"
Friends	Annual "guys" or "girls" trip
Making a difference	Donate to charity
Spirituality	Go to church or temple
Independence	Stop working
Growth	Go back to school
Creativity	Learn to paint
Adventure	Take trip to Africa
Fulfillment	Stay married
Confidence	Exercise
Balance	Plan life better
Love	Have great marriage
Health	Lose weight

FIVE-STAR TIP

If you share your life with a partner, it's best to work on your Value Circles together. That way, if either of you gets stuck, the other can act as a prompter, asking the types of questions listed above. Most important, sharing this exercise can have a positive impact on your relationship. Over the years, I have heard from many couples who've said that this exercise dramatically impacted their lives. Some of them even say it has taken their relationships to a whole new level.

Other values might include: loyalty, education, tradition, authenticity, strength of purpose, honesty, generosity, kindness, beauty, community, the environment, fairness, or intelligence. Only you know what matters deeply to you. This is your opportunity to single out five of your core values and commit to making them your focus.

If you're still stuck, try asking yourself the questions listed below. Answering them may help focus your thoughts and ideas.

ASK YOURSELF:

- **Is This a Value or a Goal?** If it's a goal, put it aside for now. You want to focus on *values only*.
- **What Does This Value Mean to Me?** Think in concrete terms—for example, "Security [a value] means to me that I can live my life without financial fears."
- **How Important Is This Value to Me?** Remember: You're working to find five *core* values. If a value occurs to you, but it isn't one that you'd stand or fall on, take it out of the circle and keep thinking.

DESIGNING YOUR PURPOSE-FOCUSED FINANCIAL PLAN™

Now that you have your values down on paper, it's time to set some specific goals for the year. These goals are the basis of your Purpose-Focused Financial Plan. In fact, a Purpose-Focused Financial Plan is nothing more than a list of things to do (your goals) to enable you to live a life in line with the values that are most important to you. Here are seven tips on how to define your goals, followed by a worksheet that will help you create your plan.

1. Base your goals on your values.

You've just completed the Value Circle, in which you identified the five values you want to focus on this year. Maybe you were skeptical about this exercise, but you're about to find out how it can transform your life. Ideally, each of your five values should lead you to a specific key goal. In your Purpose-Focused Financial Plan (page 38), you'll write down a value and then, right next to it, a related goal on which you want to focus your time and energy.

2. Make your goals specific, detailed, and with a deadline.

In order to achieve a goal, you must know precisely what it is that you're after. This process will help you take those vague ideas and thoughts about the sort of life you see for yourself and turn them into something concrete. Say one of your values is "Family." You want to spend more quality time together and your goal is to have a vacation house where you can all congregate. You could write "own a vacation house" on your worksheet, but what would that accomplish? Not much, because a general phrase like "own a vacation house" doesn't help you focus on what you need to do to accomplish your goal. On the other hand, you could ask yourself specific questions like: Where would I want this vacation house to be located? How much would it cost? What steps would I have to take to make this happen? When can I take action and begin working toward my goal? How long will it take me to make my vacation home dream a reality? Once you can answer these types of questions, your goal will start to feel real and exciting. You'll be ready to draw up a timetable that outlines the entire process of reaching your goal. The worksheet on page 38 provides five boxes designed to help you do just that—turn your goals into specific, detailed plans of action.

3. Put your top five goals in writing.

I know it's a cliché, but it also happens to be true: People who write down their financial goals get rich. Study after study has shown that writing down your goals makes it much more likely that you'll achieve them. It's a truly amazing phenomenon—the process of writing down your goals on paper does something to you subconsciously that helps make those goals more specific and real to you. When you write down your goals, you make them important. When you write down important goals, you make your life purposeful.

4. Start taking action toward your goals within 48 hours.

Writing down your goals is great, but it's not enough. You must take action, the quicker the better. That's because if you don't start moving toward your goal *now,* you may never get moving at all. You'll see that the Purpose-Focused Financial Plan worksheet includes a box that asks you to write out your 48-hour action step. This action can be anything. All that matters is that you do something to bring yourself closer to your goal. For example, if your goal is a vacation home, you could go on the Internet and start researching the housing market in your ideal destination. Remember, *what* you do in that first 48 hours is not as important as the fact that you do *something.* Your action creates positive momentum that will help carry your goal through to reality. (And don't be put off if achieving your goal will require a lot more money than you have right now. In the chapters to come, you will learn how to overcome this particular challenge and realize your dreams.)

5. Enlist help.

There's a huge myth out there that I'd like to bust: the myth of the "self-made" person. There's no such thing. No one ever reaches an important goal without some sort of help from some other person. It's part of being human. So when it comes to achieving your goals, stop and think for a second. To whom can you turn for help in achieving your top five goals? Consider family members, friends, people you work or socialize with, or people with a specific area of expertise related to your goals. As you create your Purpose-Focused Financial Plan, include a list of people whom you should enlist to help you achieve your goals.

6. Get a rough idea of how much money it will cost to achieve your goals.

As you define your top five goals, you're going to find that some may have nothing to do with money, while others are all about money. Some goals will take almost no time to save for, and others may take a lot of time and investing to reach. Since it's important to know which is which, part of creating your Purpose-Focused Financial Plan involves estimating how much money you think you will ultimately need to pay for your top five goals. So ask yourself, What is this goal going to cost? How much do I need to start putting aside each week or month to help me get there? Knowing the answers to these questions will enable you to do two things: (1) understand how realistic (or unrealistic) your goals may be, and (2) get you started on a systematic savings and investment plan to accumulate the money you are going to need to achieve them.

> ### 7. Make sure your goals match the values you share with your partner or family.

Don't keep your goals to yourself. If you have a partner or a family, it's important to make sure your goals reflect what they want, too. By discussing your values and dreams with the people in your life, you help create your future together. In fact, you can work on a family list of goals that you all want to accomplish jointly.

IT'S TIME TO GET STARTED!

Now let's get busy. Use the Purpose-Focused Financial Plan worksheet that follows to get yourself thinking about the five key things you want to accomplish over the next 12 months. Remember, your goals need to be *specific* and *measurable*. For example, you may want to pay off your credit-card debt. Or you may want to start saving for a down payment on a house. Whatever it is, you need to write it in such a way that at the end of 12 months, you'll be able to determine if you have accomplished the goal.

PURPOSE-FOCUSED FINANCIAL PLAN™
Designing a Proactive Year

The goal of a Purpose-Focused Financial Plan is to write down what you are going to focus your energy on in the next 12 months. To do this, follow the six steps below and fill in the worksheet on the following page:

1. List your top five values. Ideally you already did this when we covered the concept of creating your Value Circle. Remember you are writing down values first to address the issue of who you want to "be" as a person.

2. Based on your top five values, write down specifically what you want to "do." Your top five "to do's" will be your top five goals for the next 12 months.

3. Now it is time to make these goals specific and measurable. Remember— the more detailed and provable, the better.

4. In the fourth box on the next page, it's time to hit hard the "48-hour plan." What action can you take in the next 48 hours to move toward your goals? Remember that "I don't know" is not acceptable. The answer to "I don't know" is . . . "I know you don't, but if you did, what would you do in the next 48 hours to get moving?"

5. Who are you going to go to for help? Be specific. You will need help if your goal is big and worth going for. In this box, write in who could help you reach your goal.

6. When are you going to start and when is your deadline to finish?

PURPOSE-FOCUSED FINANCIAL PLAN™

TOP FIVE VALUES	TOP FIVE FINANCIAL GOALS	MAKE SPECIFIC, MEASURABLE, PROVABLE	48-HOUR PLAN — WHAT ACTIONS WILL YOU TAKE IN THE NEXT 48 HOURS?	ENLIST HELP — WHOM WILL YOU SHARE YOUR GOALS WITH?	START & FINISH LINE — WHEN WILL YOU START? WHEN WILL YOU FINISH?
Example SECURITY	INCREASE NET WORTH BY 10% IN 2003	INCREASE CONTRIBUTIONS TO 401(K) FROM 6% TO 12%	CALL BENEFITS PERSON AT WORK; CHANGE CONTRIBUTIONS PLAN BY FRIDAY	CALL PETE (FINANCIAL ADVISOR) TO REVIEW INVESTMENT OPTIONS IN 401(K) PLAN; ASK HIM ABOUT ROTH IRA	START TOMORROW, MONDAY, JAN. 13, 2003; FINISH BY FRIDAY, JAN. 17, 2003
1.					
2.					
3.					
4.					
5.					

You now have a Purpose-Focused Financial Plan. If you stick to it, you'll make incredible progress over the next 12 months. Now let's move on to the next exercise, which will help you make sure your spending habits are in line with your new goals.

ARE YOU LIVING RICH OR JUST EXPENSIVELY?

You've nearly completed Step 3. There is just one final exercise that will determine if the way you are currently spending money is bringing you closer to your values or pushing you farther away. I've taught this exercise to thousands of people in seminars and I've learned firsthand that almost everyone has expenses (many of them fixed monthly overhead expenses) that actually have nothing to do with their values. If you're in this situation, don't worry. You'll soon find it easy to come up with ways to reduce your overhead without feeling as if you are giving up anything. You might even come up with some new financial goals once you realize where your money is going.

How to Find Out If the Way You're Spending Money Reflects Who You Want to *Be*

Start by making a list of your last month's 10 biggest expenses on the following worksheet.

To do this accurately, go back and review your checkbook and your credit-card statements. The expenses you list could include fixed overhead costs like rent, mortgage, and utilities, or something you might do just once this year, like taking a vacation.

Once you have your top 10 list of expenses, try to determine if each of them matches a value that you feel is important. List that value under the "Value" column for each expense. Then ask yourself the question, Does this expense reflect any of my values? Write "Yes" or "No" in the last column.

How Much I Spent	Item	Core Value	Reflects My Values?
Sample Entries $500/MONTH	CLOTHING	MAKE A DIFFERENCE	NO
$2,000/MONTH	MORTGAGE PAYMENT	SECURITY	YES
1.			
2.			
3.			
4.			
5.			
6.			
7.			
8.			
9.			
10.			

If you answered no for any of these expenditures, is there a change you can make to put your spending more in line with your values?

CONGRATULATIONS!

You're well on your way to planning your finances—and your life. You've done some profound thinking about what you value and how you can make your values the basis for your financial plan.

Now that you've written out your financial values and goals, you may be wondering where you are going to find the money it will take to realize your dreams. Don't worry—the answer is just ahead.

FIND YOUR LATTE FACTOR™

THE PROBLEM IS NOT HOW MUCH WE MAKE ...
IT'S HOW MUCH WE SPEND!

If you remember only one thing from this workbook, it should be this: *How much you earn has almost no bearing on whether or not you will build wealth.* Ask anyone who got a raise last year if their savings increased. In almost every case, the answer will be no. Why? Because the more we make, the more we spend.

It's actually considered almost unpatriotic not to increase our spending when our income goes up. Unfortunately, if we keep raising our spending to match our earnings—or worse, spend more than we make—we wind up in a never-ending rat race. We're working hard with almost nothing to show for it, because at the end of the month the money is already spent. This is called living paycheck to paycheck, and it's a vicious cycle you don't want to fall into. When you spend more than you make, you subject yourself to a life of stress, fear, debt, and a future of poverty—or, even worse, bankruptcy.

THE LATTE FACTOR CAN MAKE YOU RICH

What do most Americans do with the money they earn? They waste a lot of it every day—mainly on "small things." I put quotation marks around "small things" because the phrase is misleading. The so-called "small things" on which we spend so much can add up in a hurry to amazingly large amounts of money.

It doesn't have to be this way. Most of us don't really think about how we spend our money—or if we do, we focus solely on the big items. At the same time, we ignore the small but steady expenses that drain away our cash. We don't think about what it costs us to earn our money and we don't realize how much wealth we could have if, instead of wasting our income, we invested it.

By understanding what I call The Latte Factor, you're going to change all that. You're going to become aware of the ways that small amounts of money spent daily can add up to a fortune spent over your lifetime. You're also going to learn how to control your expenditures so you can save a portion of every single dollar you earn. This is crucial, for no matter how big your paycheck is, if you don't save, you will never live a life of financial abundance. By the same token, no matter how small your paycheck happens to be, if you save consistently (even if it's just a little at a time), you can finish rich. The point is, you work hard for your money, and your money should work just as hard for you!

What's The Latte Factor™?

The Latte Factor is a simple concept that evolved from something a young woman told me at one of my FinishRich seminars. I'd been talking about the importance of putting away $5 to $10 a day to save for retirement. Well, Kim was living from paycheck to paycheck, and insisted that she couldn't even manage $50 a month. "I'm in debt," she said, "and I'm barely making it." So I challenged her to prove that she didn't have the money to invest. I asked her to take me through an average day.

"Well," she said, "I go to work and then I research——"

"Do you start your day with coffee?" I asked.

It quickly came out that she did, and in fact, it wasn't coffee from home or from the office.

"I go downstairs and buy a latte every morning," she told me.

"Do you buy a single or a double latte?" I asked.

"I always buy a double nonfat latte."

"Great," I said. "What does this double nonfat latte cost you every morning?"

"About $3.50."

"Do you just buy the latte, or do you also get a muffin or a bagel with that?"

"I usually get a muffin."

"What does that muffin cost?" I asked

"I guess about $1.50."

"How can a muffin cost $1.50?"

Kim explained it was fat-free.

"So you're spending about $5 a day for a latte and a fat-free muffin. . . . Interesting."

I let Kim continue taking me through her day, and in the process we found another $10 in miscellaneous costs—a candy bar here, a Power Bar there, a protein shake in the afternoon, and so on. It turned out that by making her own coffee or by cutting out a couple of diet Cokes and candy bars, she could save about $5 a day, which equaled roughly $150 a month, or almost $2,000 a year. Kim could put this amount in her company's retirement plan and let it grow tax-free until she retired. If she put in $2,000 every year, and she invested it all in stocks (which have averaged an 11 percent growth rate a year over the last 50 years), by the time she reached 65, she would probably have more than *$2 million* sitting in her account. She could retire a multimillionaire!

When Kim saw the number "$2 million," her immediate response was "David, are you trying to tell me my lattes are costing me millions of dollars?"

Everyone in the class looked at her and, in unison, said, "YES!"

Now there are a lot of ways to attack this Latte Factor attitude. I've had critics say, "But where am I going to make 11 percent a year on my money? We're never going to see those kinds of returns happen again." I've learned not to argue with these people. Cut the 11 percent annual return in half and assume you'll earn only 5.5 percent a year. You'll still end up with tens of thousands of dollars in savings—maybe hundreds of thousands in savings, depending on your age and how early you got started.

The point of The Latte Factor is that everyone makes enough money to become rich. What keeps us living from paycheck to paycheck is that we spend more than we make on stuff we don't need. The amount you are throwing away on junk food and other non-essential goods is your Latte Factor. If you were to take that money and devote it to savings, you'd soon be putting away 12 percent of what you earn. Before you know it, your life would have changed for the better.

"A Latte Spurned Is a Fortune Earned"
—*People Weekly*

In 2001, *People* magazine published a feature story about my Latte Factor concept. This simple idea is now recognized internationally as a metaphor for how we waste money. If you look around, you'll see it happening everywhere. Try this: Visit your local coffee shop for just one hour some morning and count the number of people buying coffee. If it's a fancy franchise like, say, Starbucks, a cappuccino will cost about $3.50. Just think what that daily cup of coffee adds up to over time for each of those folks! Now check out the math:

A Latte a Day Keeps Retirement Away

Buy a latte every day and here's what you will spend:

A Latte a Day = $3.50
A Latte a Day for a Week = $24.50
A Latte a Day for a Month = $105
A Latte a Day for a Year = $1,260
A Latte a Day for a Decade = $12,600

I joined Barbara Walters recently on *The View* and did this math for the audience. When I had finished, I said very simply, "If you're going to buy a coffee every day at Starbucks, for goodness' sake, at least also buy the stock." The audience laughed. Now, understand that I'm not really recommending Starbucks stock. And truthfully, I don't mean to pick on Starbucks. I happen to enjoy their coffee myself. The Latte Factor is a metaphor that illustrates how we spend money without realizing what it adds up to. You might be spending more than you need to on items like cigarettes, bottled water, cola, or candy bars. The sooner you find out what your Latte Factor is and change your ways, the sooner you will have the extra money you need to save a fortune.

Consider this:

USE THE POWER OF THE LATTE FACTOR

$3.50 (average cost of a latte) × 7 days a week = $24.50

If you invested $24.50 a week and earned a 10% annual rate of return, you'd wind up with:

1 year	$1,339
2 years	$2,818
5 years	$8,257
10 years	$21,870
15 years	$44,314
30 years	$242,916

Here's another way to look at it: If you spent just $1 less a day on coffee and instead put that money in a good investment program, how much money could you make?

A Dollar a Day Can Grow Up to Be $1 Million . . .

Here's what happens if you start making a dollar a day work for you.

> $1 a day at 5%   = $1 million in 99 years (too long . . . won't work)
>
> $1 a day at 10% = $1 million in 56 years
>
> $1 a day at 15% = $1 million in 40 years

For the moment, don't worry about where you are going to get annual returns of 10 or 15 percent. We'll cover that in detail in Step Eight. Let's just assume that you probably can afford to invest more than $1 a day. So let's see what happens if you invest a little bit more.

$10 Can Turn into $1 Million a Lot Faster Than $1 . . .

This is a fact: If you can manage to save $10 a day, you can get rich. All you need to do to become wealthy is commit right now to putting a fixed amount of money every day in growth investments.

> $10 a day at 5%   = $1 million in 54 years (still doesn't work great)
>
> $10 a day at 10% = $1 million in 34 years
>   (not quite so bad . . . we're getting there)
>
> $10 a day at 15% = $1 million in 25 years
>   (that's really just around the corner)

If you're part of a couple, and you and your partner *both* saved $10 a day, look at what would happen:

> $20 a day at 10% = $1 million in 27 years
>
> $20 a day at 15% = $1 million in 21 years

There are no tricks here. Becoming rich simply requires committing and sticking to a systematic savings and investment plan. We'll talk more about how to do that in Step 8. For now, I want you to focus on the fact that you don't need to have a lot of money to make a lot of money. You just need to make the right decisions and act on them. Need more inspiration? The chart below shows how to build real wealth by investing only $3.33, $5.00, or $6.66 a day.

TO BUILD WEALTH . . . FIND YOUR LATTE FACTOR AND START SAVING MONTHLY						
Your Monthly Investment	Your Age	Total Amount of Monthly Investments Through Age 65	At a 4% Rate of Return	At a 7% Rate of Return	At a 9% Rate of Return	At a 12% Rate of Return
$100	25	48,000	118,590	264,012	471,643	1,188,242
	30	42,000	91,678	181,156	296,385	649,527
	40	30,000	51,584	81,480	112,953	189,764
	50	18,000	24,691	31,881	38,124	50,458
$150	25	72,000	177,294	393,722	702,198	1,764,716
	30	63,000	137,060	270,158	441,268	964,644
	40	45,000	77,119	121,511	168,168	281,827
	50	27,000	36,914	47,544	56,761	74,937
$200	25	96,000	237,180	528,025	943,286	2,376,484
	30	84,000	183,355	362,312	592,770	1,299,054
	40	60,000	103,169	162,959	225,906	379,527
	50	36,000	49,382	63,762	76,249	100,915

Get Your Spending Under Control

Now let's find your Latte Factor. Again, don't be tempted to skip any part of the following exercises. This step may lead to the single most significant life change you make for your financial future. You're going to discover how to make your income go far enough so you can finish rich. We'll begin by figuring out just how much money you could be putting away if you simply used the Latte Factor to your advantage.

> ## EXERCISE NO. 1
> ### Know What You Earn

This exercise should be easy because you can get most of the information you need from the "Where Does Your Money Really Go?" assignment in Step 2 (pages 19–22). Look back at that worksheet and find the figures to plug into the following sentence:

I currently earn $_____ a month before taxes, and $_____ after taxes.

> ## EXERCISE NO. 2
> ### Estimate What You Spend Each Month

Are you beginning to see how essential all the work you've done so far really is? Because you established the facts of your current financial situation in Step 2, you now have an enormous amount of vital information at your fingertips. So once again, turn to the "Where Does Your Money Really Go?" assignment in Step 2 (page 22) for the figures you'll need to fill in the blanks below.

I currently spend $_____ a month.

Now subtract your monthly spending total from your monthly after-tax income.

How much I earn each month after taxes $_____

How much I spend each month (approximately)   − $_____

My monthly cash flow   = $_____

Is your cash flow positive or negative? Your goal, obviously, is to have a positive cash flow—that is, to earn more than you spend every month. If you're already doing that, good for you! The following exercises will help you save even more and allow you to reach your goals even faster. If you have a negative cash flow, you're spending more money than you're earning—and robbing yourself of a rich future in the process. The next four exercises will help you get your cash flowing in a positive direction.

EXERCISE NO. 3
Track What You Really Spend

Although we now know how much you spend every month, we still don't have a good picture of where exactly that money is going. It's time to figure out your everyday spending habits. Starting tomorrow, I want you to record every single penny you spend for the next seven days. Carry this workbook with you for one week and record in it every penny you spend. Write down every purchase you make, no matter how big or small. (I mean *everything*: highway tolls, candy bars, late fees on library books—everything.)

Once you've captured your spending habits on paper, you'll quickly see where you're wasting your money. Every evening, enter the expenses that represent wasted money onto the following chart.

This Seven-Day Financial Challenge™ can be a lot of fun as well as very informative. But for it to work you must promise me—and yourself—two things. (1) You'll write down everything you spend. That means you won't leave *anything* out. (2) You won't suddenly change your spending habits because you're embarrassed about what you might find. Spend money in exactly the way you usually do.

One more thing: If you have a spouse or significant other, photocopy the section below and get him or her to try the challenge also. Then compare notes at the end of the week.

THE SEVEN-DAY FINANCIAL CHALLENGE™

MONDAY

Item	Cost	Wasted Money? (✓ for Yes)
_____	$ _____	_____
_____	$ _____	_____
_____	$ _____	_____
_____	$ _____	_____
_____	$ _____	_____
_____	$ _____	_____
_____	$ _____	_____
_____	$ _____	_____
_____	$ _____	_____
_____	$ _____	_____
_____	$ _____	_____
_____	$ _____	

Total Daily Latte Factor (total of checked items) $ _____

TUESDAY

Item	Cost	Wasted Money? (✓ for Yes)
_____	$ _____	_____
_____	$ _____	_____
_____	$ _____	_____
_____	$ _____	_____
_____	$ _____	_____
_____	$ _____	_____
_____	$ _____	_____
_____	$ _____	_____
_____	$ _____	_____
_____	$ _____	_____
_____	$ _____	_____
_____	$ _____	_____

Total Daily Latte Factor (total of checked items) $ _____

THE SEVEN-DAY FINANCIAL CHALLENGE™

WEDNESDAY

Item	Cost	Wasted Money? (✓ for Yes)
_____	$ _____	_____
_____	$ _____	_____
_____	$ _____	_____
_____	$ _____	_____
_____	$ _____	_____
_____	$ _____	_____
_____	$ _____	_____
_____	$ _____	_____
_____	$ _____	_____
_____	$ _____	_____
_____	$ _____	_____
_____	$ _____	
_____	$ _____	

Total Daily Latte Factor (total of checked items) $ _____

THURSDAY

Item	Cost	Wasted Money? (✓ for Yes)
_____	$ _____	_____
_____	$ _____	_____
_____	$ _____	_____
_____	$ _____	_____
_____	$ _____	_____
_____	$ _____	_____
_____	$ _____	_____
_____	$ _____	_____
_____	$ _____	_____
_____	$ _____	_____
_____	$ _____	_____
_____	$ _____	
_____	$ _____	

Total Daily Latte Factor (total of checked items) $ _____

THE SEVEN-DAY FINANCIAL CHALLENGE™

FRIDAY

Item	Cost	Wasted Money? (✓ for Yes)
_____	$ _____	_____
_____	$ _____	_____
_____	$ _____	_____
_____	$ _____	_____
_____	$ _____	_____
_____	$ _____	_____
_____	$ _____	_____
_____	$ _____	_____
_____	$ _____	_____
_____	$ _____	_____
_____	$ _____	_____
_____	$ _____	_____

Total Daily Latte Factor (total of checked items) $ _____

SATURDAY

Item	Cost	Wasted Money? (✓ for Yes)
_____	$ _____	_____
_____	$ _____	_____
_____	$ _____	_____
_____	$ _____	_____
_____	$ _____	_____
_____	$ _____	_____
_____	$ _____	_____
_____	$ _____	_____
_____	$ _____	_____
_____	$ _____	_____
_____	$ _____	_____
_____	$ _____	_____

Total Daily Latte Factor (total of checked items) $ _____

THE SEVEN-DAY FINANCIAL CHALLENGE™

SUNDAY

Item	Cost	Wasted Money? (✓ for Yes)
_____	$ _____	_____
_____	$ _____	_____
_____	$ _____	_____
_____	$ _____	_____
_____	$ _____	_____
_____	$ _____	_____
_____	$ _____	_____
_____	$ _____	_____
_____	$ _____	_____
_____	$ _____	_____
_____	$ _____	_____
_____	$ _____	

Total Daily Latte Factor (total of checked items) $ _____

NOW ADD UP THE SEVEN DAILY TOTALS

This is your ...

TOTAL WEEKLY LATTE FACTOR $ _____

Now multiply the weekly factor by 52 (the number of weeks in a year) to find your ...

TOTAL YEARLY LATTE FACTOR $ _____

You see how the money adds up? It will add up just as significantly on the positive side of your financial future as soon as you put The Latte Factor to work for you.

EXERCISE NO. 4
Start Paying Cash

Now that you've tracked a typical week's expenses, are you ready to start changing your ways? The easiest thing you can do to reduce your spending automatically is to commit to paying for everything with cash.

When you buy things with credit cards or personal checks, you don't feel the significance of your spending. Your mind plays tricks on you. You haven't actually handed over the green stuff, so you don't quite believe that you're spending money. I dare you to stick $500 in cash in your wallet and try to spend it frivolously on impulse purchases. You'll have a hard time doing it. That's because cash makes you think about exactly how much you are spending and for what. I can't tell you how many of my FinishRich readers have told me that when they went to a cash-only system, their spending dropped by 20 percent in a single month!

To get you started, review your checkbook register (if you actually record stuff—a lot of people don't) and your credit-card statements for the last month. Make a list on the following page of the items that you bought. Figure out which of those items it would have been smarter to pay for with cash. Put a check mark next to those items.

MY NONCASH SPENDING		
Item	**Amount**	**Smarter to Pay with Cash? (✓ for Yes)**
_____	$ _____	_____
_____	$ _____	_____
_____	$ _____	_____
_____	$ _____	_____
_____	$ _____	_____
_____	$ _____	_____
_____	$ _____	_____
_____	$ _____	_____
_____	$ _____	_____
_____	$ _____	_____
_____	$ _____	_____
_____	$ _____	_____
_____	$ _____	_____
_____	$ _____	_____
_____	$ _____	_____
_____	$ _____	_____
_____	$ _____	_____
_____	$ _____	_____
_____	$ _____	_____
_____	$ _____	_____
_____	$ _____	_____

What was your total spending for credit-card and check purchases last month? $ _____

Now try to single out *at least half* of the items on your list and commit to paying for them with cash in the future.

After a week of paying for the checked items in cash, take the next step: check off half of the remaining items on your list, and pay cash for them, too. In the third week, make it your goal to check off the remaining items and use cash for all your purchases. You'll be amazed at how your spending declines.

See what I mean? Keep going! You're on your way to letting The Latte Factor change your future!

> **EXERCISE NO. 5**
> **Give Yourself a Credit-Card Haircut**

You're finally getting a handle on your spending, which is great. Nothing is more productive or exciting in your financial life than to finally take control of your finances. Conversely, as we've seen, nothing produces more stress or robs your future more than out-of-control spending.

This exercise is a symbolic lesson in taking control and putting yourself on the road to a rich future. Right now, pull out all your credit-card bills for this month. List each card below, and beside it write in the total amount due.

Credit-Card Company	Amount Owed
	$
	$
	$
	$
	$
	$
	$
	$
	$
	$
	$
	$
	$
	$
	$
	$

Take a red pen and circle the card on which you owe the most. Then find that card in your wallet, remove it, and cut it up. Trust me, the feeling of power you get from this small token gesture can be tremendous. Just try it. Remember, of course, to keep paying the bills. If need be, you can always call the card company and order a replacement card.

Don't you feel great? You've just successfully eliminated another means of overspending. If you think you can handle it, keep going and cut up more than one card. If you have more credit-card debt than you want (and who doesn't?), keep reading, because in the next step we are going to cover in detail how to get out of credit-card debt and repair your credit record if you have a problem.

> ### EXERCISE NO. 6
> ### Never Spend More Than $100 on Anything
> ### Without Taking 48 Hours to Think About It

The idea behind this exercise is simple. Most Americans spend far too much money on purchases they really don't need to make. Temptation is everywhere. Stores, catalogs, online shopping sites, and television shopping channels are all designed to get you caught up in the excitement of shopping, so that before you know what's happened, you've bought something. This is called "impulse buying," and it can be a real disease. To vaccinate yourself against it, set yourself a spending ceiling. I suggest $100, but it can be any amount that makes sense to you. Once you've set your ceiling, do not permit yourself to buy *anything* for that amount or above without first taking 48 hours to think about it. The two-day "cooling-off" period allows you to decide rationally whether the purchase is really necessary.

For the next month I want you to track the items that you put "on hold" because they exceed your ceiling. List them in the spaces on the following page. Put a check mark only next to the items you decided to buy after thinking about it for 48 hours.

Item over $100	Purchased? (✓)
_____	_____
_____	_____
_____	_____
_____	_____
_____	_____
_____	_____
_____	_____
_____	_____
_____	_____
_____	_____
_____	_____
_____	_____
_____	_____
_____	_____
_____	_____
_____	_____
_____	_____
_____	_____
_____	_____
_____	_____

IT'S TIME TO GIVE YOURSELF THAT PAY CUT!

Now that you've seen all the ways that you can make The Latte Factor work for you, why not take control of your own destiny and create your future now? Remember that the whole point of The Latte Factor is to increase your rate of saving. Review what you've recorded in the seven exercises you just completed. Then use that vital information to put The Latte Factor to work below.

(a) I earn monthly before taxes $_____

(b) I currently save monthly $_____

Now let's determine your current rate of savings and your ideal rate of savings.

To find your current rate of savings, divide the amount you save each month by the amount you earn each month. (For example, if you earn $1,000 a month before taxes and save $100 a month, your savings rate is 0.1, or 10 percent.)

$_____ ÷ $_____ × 100 = _____%

(My monthly savings)   *(My monthly earnings)*   *(My savings rate)*

Ideally, you should aim to save at least 10 percent of your monthly gross income. So let's determine how much that figure is in dollars. To do this, multiply your monthly gross income by 0.1. (For example, if your monthly income is $3,500, a 10 percent contribution to long-term savings would equal $350 per month.)

My ideal 10-percent solution to finishing rich is

$_____ × 0.1 = $_____

(monthly income)   (ideal savings)

You now know what your new savings goal should be. In Step 6, we'll show you where to put all the money you'll be accumulating.

CONGRATULATIONS!

You've successfully identified the ways in which you can take control of your spending and boost your rate of saving. Doesn't it feel good to finally be in a position to tackle the debts you're carrying? It's great to know you're building critical momentum toward a rich future.

THE DEBT-FREE SOLUTION™:
GET OUT OF DEBT . . .
AND STAY OUT OF DEBT

One of the most important keys to living smart and finishing rich is leading what I call a "Debt-Free Lifestyle." These days, however, doing this can be a real challenge. According to a recent *USA Today* article, by the time the average college student gets out of school, he or she has three credit cards and is close to $3,000 in debt. For adults, the figures are worse . . . much worse. All told, American families currently owe a total of roughly half a *trillion* dollars in credit-card debt. That works out to nearly $8,400 per household. It's truly a war out there—and the credit-card companies are winning.

In this chapter, you're going to learn a series of concrete steps that will enable you to regain control of your finances. Specifically, I am going to share with you a 13-point action plan designed to get you out of credit-card debt. I am also going to show you how to protect your credit record. And, finally, I'll provide you with letters to send to the credit-card companies and agencies that track your credit records in the event you find errors.

EVEN "BLACK BELT" SHOPPERS CAN GET OUT OF DEBT!

If it sometimes seems as if you are drowning in credit-card debt, believe me—I know how you feel. I've been there. You know how some people get black belts in karate? Well, I used to have a black belt in shopping.

If you've read my previous books, you know that when I was a freshman at the University of Southern California, one of the first things I did was sign up for a bunch of credit cards. I couldn't help myself. When I registered for my dorm room the first day at school, right next to the student ID table was another table where some people were giving away "free gifts" (like clock radios, dictionaries, and bike locks). All you had to do to get one was sign up for a credit card. So I did.

Of course, I told myself I'd use these cards only for "emergencies." Funny thing, though—emergencies turned out to be easy to have.

Pretty soon, I was going on weekly shopping trips that left me owing thousands of dollars in credit-card debt. I remember being so upset by my credit-card bills that I would literally get dizzy when I opened them up each month. It took me the better part of two years to get myself out of the debt hole I had dug for myself, but I managed to do it—and so can you.

What follows is a step-by-step action plan designed to get you out of debt and repair your credit record if you have a problem. It's exactly what I would advise you to do if I were to come to your house and personally coach you.

A 13-STEP ACTION PLAN TO GET OUT OF CREDIT-CARD DEBT

> ### STEP ONE
> ### Determine if you have a credit-card problem.

There are many different rules of thumb to determine if you have a credit-card problem. Some experts insist that if you are making only the minimum payments on your credit-card bills, you definitely have a problem. Other experts use formulas like the one that says that you're in trouble if you're spending more than 20 percent of your income paying off credit-card debt. Then there is Steve Rhode, the founder of the nationally recognized debt-counseling organization MyVesta.org. In his view, if you think you have a problem, then you do.

I happen to agree with Rhode. When it comes to debt, there aren't any simple rules or formulas. The guideline you should use is how you feel about your situation.

So how do you feel?

The following simple exercise will help you figure this out.

To begin with, get out all your credit cards and all your credit-card statements and put them on the dining room table. (If you are married or have a partner, try to get them to do the same with their cards and statements.) Now fill in the following blanks to . . .

FIGURE OUT HOW MANY CARDS YOU HAVE

I have _____ [fill in the number] credit cards.

My spouse/partner has _____ credit cards.

My kids (or other dependents living with me) have _____ credit cards.

Taken together, the whole family has _____ credit cards.

Now list each credit-card account and its current outstanding balance, starting with the largest debt and working down to the smallest. In this way, you will . . .

. . . FIGURE OUT HOW MUCH YOU OWE				
Name of Creditor	Account Number	Outstanding Balance	Monthly Minimum Payment	Interest Rate
1.				
2.				
3.				
4.				
5.				

...FIGURE OUT HOW MUCH YOU OWE				
Name of Creditor	Account Number	Outstanding Balance	Monthly Minimum Payment	Interest Rate
6.				
7.				
8.				
9.				
10.				
11.				
12.				
13.				

The total amount of debt on these cards is $ _____

The total monthly minimum payment due is $ _____

Now that you know how many cards you have and how much credit-card debt you have, indicate whether you feel the following statements are true or false.

T ❑ F ❑   I have too many credit cards.

T ❑ F ❑   I'm carrying too much debt.

T ❑ F ❑   I'm comfortable with how many credit cards I have and the amount of debt I'm carrying.

T ❑ F ❑   I'm still not sure how I feel.

(If your answer to the last statement is "true," ask yourself what you would say if you *were* sure.)

```
┌────────────────────────────────────────────────┐
│                   STEP TWO                      │
│         Pay down your debt systematically.      │
└────────────────────────────────────────────────┘
```

The best way I know of to pay off credit-card debt is what I call the Debt-Free Solution™.

The Debt-Free Solution™ is about momentum. It's about getting all your cards, one after another, "gone." By "gone," I mean you've paid off the balance you owed and you have closed the account. In other words, gone.

If you want to keep a card or two for emergency purposes or to build a credit record, that's fine. But the rest of your plastic is going to be DOLP™— which stands for Dead On Last Payment.

So let's get DOLPing!

The first thing you do is take out all your credit-card statements and calculate their DOLP numbers. Here's how you do that. Take the current outstanding balance on each statement and divide it by the minimum payment that particular card company wants from you. The result is that account's DOLP number.

For example, say your outstanding Visa balance is $500 and they want a $50 minimum payment. Dividing the total debt ($500) by the minimum payment ($50) gives you a DOLP number of 10.

Once you've figured out the DOLP number for each account, rank them in reverse order. In other words, the account with the lowest DOLP number is first, the one with the second-lowest number is second, and so on. The table below shows what your list should look like.

THE DOLP™ SYSTEM: CREATING A STRATEGY TO PAY DOWN DEBT

Account	Outstanding Balance	Monthly Minimum Payment	DOLP Number	DOLP Ranking
Visa	$500	$50	10	1
MasterCard	$775	$65	12	2
Sears Card	$1,150	$35	39	3

By creating this list, you now know which credit card can be paid off the fastest by making minimum payments. Now, does this mean you should make only minimum payments? Absolutely not! Ideally, your payments should be a lot higher than the minimum. How much higher? That depends on how much you can afford.

Whatever you can afford to pay above your total required minimum payments for the month should be applied to the card with the lowest-ranking DOLP. In the example above, this would be Visa. Every penny you can afford to pay beyond the total required minimum should go into that card until you've DOLPed it. Then you would focus on the card whose DOLP ranking is 2—in this case, MasterCard.

You should continue doing this until you've DOLPed your way to being debt-free. This is the Debt-Free Solution™.

Seems easy, right? Well, it's not. It may take you months, maybe even years, to pay off all your credit-card debt. But the Debt-Free Solution™ *is* simple in that it allows you to figure out the most efficient order to pay off your cards.

Many experts will suggest that you pay off your cards in a different order, one based on the interest rate each card charges. I disagree. As I'll show you later, it's actually quite easy to get a credit-card company to lower the interest rate it charges you on your debt. If you do this correctly, you should end up with pretty much the same interest rate on all your accounts. So try my DOLP system, and get debt-free.

Below is a table you can use to work out your DOLP rankings.

Account	Outstanding Balance	Monthly Minimum Payment	DOLP Number (Outstanding Balance divided by Minimum Monthly Payment)	DOLP Ranking (Lowest DOLP number is ranked #1)

> **STEP THREE**
> **Get your credit-card company to lower your interest rate.**

There's an amazingly simple way to make paying off your credit-card debt easier: Just call your credit-card company and ask for a lower interest rate.

Go back and take a look at the first step in this exercise, where you listed your credit cards. Did you write down what interest rate you are being charged on your credit-card balances? How are you doing? Are you paying too much interest?

As I write this, the average U.S. credit card charges an annualized interest rate of just under 20 percent. What's amazing about this is that you can easily get new credit cards with rates of 10 to 15 percent, and many companies offer rates below 10 percent. To find out the current rates being offered nationwide, go to **www.bankrate.com** or look in *USA Today* or *The Wall Street Journal.*

CALL YOUR CREDIT-CARD COMPANY TODAY

Here's how to go about getting your credit-card company to give you a lower interest rate.

First, call the company and ask them to tell you your current effective annual rate. Don't be confused if they quote a rate "over prime"—as in, "Your rate is just 9 percent over prime." This doesn't mean your rate is 9 percent; it means your rate is 9 percent *plus* whatever the so-called prime lending rate happens to be. As of this writing, the prime is at 4.75 percent—which would make your effective annual rate 13.75 percent.

Once you know your real rate, ask to speak with a supervisor. Do not— I repeat, do not—ever try to negotiate a lower rate with the first person who answers the phone. Explain to the supervisor that you just received a new credit-card application from a competing company that is offering a much lower interest rate—and that unless he can match or beat the competitor's rate, you intend to transfer your balance today. The credit-card business has become so competitive that in most cases the supervisor will agree to lower your rate on the spot. It's been my experience that if you're currently paying around 20 percent, you should have no trouble getting your rate lowered to less than 14 percent.

FIVE-STAR TIP

When you call a credit-card company and ask to speak to a supervisor, you should be aware that there are often many levels of supervisors. So if the supervisor you get the first time around doesn't give you what you want, ask to speak to that supervisor's manager. And don't forget to get everyone's name. If you're told company policy forbids giving out last names, ask for an identification number. Not only will this enable you to keep track of whom you spoke to, it will also make the customer-service people wary of offending you. Generally speaking, as long as you are polite and reasonable, they will probably try their best to satisfy your request because ultimately they want to keep your business.

Another way to get a credit-card company to lower your interest rate is to offer to consolidate all of your credit-card debt with them. Consolidating your debt at one company is generally a good idea. If nothing else, it means less paperwork for you, since now you have only one credit-card company to deal with (and write checks to), making it that much easier to focus on getting debt-free. Doing this can be as easy as calling your credit-card company and reporting that you just received an offer to consolidate all your credit-card debt on a competitor's card. Tell them that the competitor is offering you a lower rate, but add that if they can match the offer, you'll consolidate your credit with them. Again, make sure to speak with a supervisor when you do this.

> ### STEP FOUR
> ### Run your credit report.

Now that you've taken an overall look at your debt situation, you need to go deeper. The best way to do that is to have a credit report run on yourself. A credit report is like a report card on your financial behavior. But a bad score on your credit report can be a lot worse than bad grades in school. When you apply for a mortgage so you can buy a home, the banks will never ask you what your GPA was in high school or college. But they will instantly run a credit report on you to find out what kind of financial grades you've been getting. Your financial grade is what's known as your credit rating, and if it's bad, you may wind up having to pay thousands of dollars a year in higher interest payments. If it's terrible, you may not get the loan at all.

HOW TO FIND OUT WHAT'S IN YOUR CREDIT REPORT

There are three main companies that keep track of consumer debt and assign credit ratings—Equifax, Experian, and TransUnion. As of this writing, all three will provide you with a preliminary report on your creditworthiness for about $9. (If you have been denied credit in the last 60 days and believe it is due to an inaccurate credit report, you can get your report for free.)

To get a copy of your report, you should contact the companies directly.

Equifax Information Services, LLC
P.O. Box 740241
Atlanta, GA   30374
www.equifax.com
Helpful phone numbers:
1-800-685-1111 (to order your credit report)
1-888-766-0008 (to place a Fraud Alert in your credit file)

Experian
P.O. Box 2104
Allen, TX   75013-2104
www.experian.com
Helpful phone numbers:
1-888-397-3742 (to order your credit report by phone or to report fraud)
1-888-397-3742 (to request a copy of your report by mail)

TransUnion Corporation
Consumer Disclosure Center
P.O. Box 1000
Chester, PA   19022
www.tuc.com
Helpful phone numbers:
1-800-888-4213 (to order your credit report)
1-800-916-8800 (to review your TUC report with a customer-service representative)

In addition to providing credit reports, the Web sites of all three companies offer a variety of services for consumers, including glossaries of credit terms,

FIVE-STAR TIP

Before you send a request in writing to any of these companies, check its Web site or make a phone call to make sure the mailing address is still current. For some reason, they seem to change their P.O. boxes all the time.

articles about managing credit, tips for protecting your ID, and explanations to help you understand your credit score.

> **STEP FIVE**
> **Scrutinize your credit report for**
> **any and all mistakes.**

A little-known secret about credit reports is that they are often filled with errors. Here are some examples of the kinds of mistakes that show up on credit reports all the time:

1. Your name, address, or phone number is wrong or out of date.

2. Your Social Security number is wrong.

3. Your birth date is wrong.

4. Your marital status is wrong or out of date.

5. Your payment record is wrong. (A credit-card company may claim you made a payment late when, in fact, you made it on time. This happens all the time, and if it's not corrected, it can actually hurt you and your credit record.)

6. Credit accounts you consider closed are listed as still being open. (This often happens when you haven't used an account in years but never "officially" closed it. Since having too many open accounts can hurt your credit score, you should always make a point of formally canceling credit accounts you no longer use. You do this by contacting the company directly and asking it to close your account and notify the credit-reporting agencies. When I first ran my own report, it showed me having about a dozen accounts—most of them from my "black belt" shopping days. Even though I hadn't used most of these accounts in years, I had to go back and get them officially closed.)

7. You are listed as having credit cards that you never applied for. (This is usually the result of fraud—something that, unfortunately, is happening more and more these days. This is one reason why it's so critical to run these reports on yourself at least once a year.)

> **STEP SIX**
> **Know your legal rights.**

If you have credit-card debt, you have basic rights that are guaranteed under the law. In particular, there are two laws you should know about: the Federal Fair Credit Reporting Act and the Federal Fair Debt Collection Practice Act.

The Federal Fair Credit Reporting Act

This act requires the credit agencies listed earlier to provide you with a free credit report in the event you are denied credit based on your report. You have 60 days from the time you find out you've been denied credit to make a written request for your report.

The law also says that if you find errors in your report and notify the credit agency of them, the agency must respond to your complaint within 30 days. What's more, if it turns out that the information it has was wrong, the agency must either correct it or delete it from your record.

The Federal Fair Debt Collection Practice Act

If you are behind in your payments, this is a law you want to know about. It was enacted specifically to stop the credit-card companies from unfairly harassing you.

This act is very clear. Among other things, it forbids debt collectors from contacting you directly without your permission. If you don't feel like talking to them, you can require them to speak with your attorney. Debtors are also forbidden to call you before 8 A.M. or after 9 P.M. And if you instruct debt collectors not to call you again, the law says they can't! Instead, they have to communicate with you in writing. What's more, they are not allowed to threaten you by suggesting that they will raise the interest rate on your debt or add special debt-collection fees.

HOW TO STOP THE HARASSMENT

If you are currently being harassed, this law provides you with remedies. Go online to www.ftc.gov to find instructions on how to inform the authorities that your rights are being violated. You should also send a letter to the debt collector who is harassing you. Here's what it should say:

Dear _____ [insert debt collector's name]:

I am writing to you to inform you that your agency, _____ [insert collection agency's name], is violating my rights under the Federal Fair Debt Collection Protection Act.

The violation[s] occurred on _____ [insert dates]. They consisted of the following: [provide brief description of the harassment].

I am requesting that you immediately cease this harassment and violation of my rights. I am sending a copy of this letter to the Attorney General of _____ [insert your home state] and the Federal Trade Commission.

Sincerely,

CC: State Attorney General
Federal Trade Commission

STEP SEVEN
If you find a mistake, challenge it.

The information in your credit report is not set in stone—especially if it's wrong. Not only are the credit-reporting agencies usually willing to correct mistakes, they are legally obligated to do so when you point them out. Here's what to do to get a credit report fixed if you find a mistake:

1. Credit reports come with what's called a "request of investigation" form. If you believe there are inaccuracies in your report, fill out this form and send it to the address indicated on it. When you send in your request of investigation, make sure to accompany it with written proof of the inaccuracy you are disputing (e.g., receipts, canceled checks, proof of payment, etc.)

2. At the same time, you should also write a letter to the company whose charge you are disputing, and send a copy to the credit agency. For example, when Michelle and I first ran our own credit reports, we found that Michelle's credit record contained a report from a hotel that claimed she had an unpaid bill of less than $200 from six years earlier. So we contacted the hotel, sorted out the error, and then followed up with the credit agency (providing them with all the necessary documentation) to get the error off her credit report. (Even though it involved only a small amount of money, it was worth the trouble, since nothing hurts your credit rating worse than unpaid bills.)

3. Watch the calendar. By law, the credit bureau must complete its investigation within 30 days of receiving your written request. Have a follow-up letter ready to go out on Day 31 if the problem has not been solved (sample letters can be found starting on page 78).

FIVE-STAR TIP

I'm not going to mislead you. Clearing up credit report errors takes time and can be a headache. It took Michelle and me about a full year to get our credit reports cleaned up, and we had a pretty straightforward situation—more than a dozen "dead accounts" listed as still open and about a half-dozen other errors. Trust me on this—making sure your credit report is accurate is worth the time and effort, because an inaccurate report can cancel out years of hard work and planning.

STEP EIGHT
Find out your FICO score.

Fair, Isaac & Co. is a little-known firm based in San Rafael, California, that has developed the most influential credit-rating system around. What they do is take your credit reports and, based on such factors as your payment history, how much you owe, and how long you've been borrowing, assign you a number. This number—known as your FICO score—can be used by anyone who is trying to decide whether they should loan you money. FICO scores range from 300 (really bad credit) to 850 (ideal borrower). About 720 is average—which is to say, pretty solid. While FICO is not the only credit-scoring system in use, it is the most widely used, playing a role in three out of every four U.S. credit applications.

Until recently, FICO scores were secret. Only lenders had access to them. But these days Fair, Isaac is a bit more forthcoming. If you go to www.MyFico.com, you can purchase 30-day access to your FICO report for $12.95. Even more important, the firm offers information on how to improve your FICO score. It may strike you as funny that this firm can score us, then sell us our score, and then offer us tips on how to improve our score. But there's no getting around it—FICO scores have an impact on your ability to get the mortgage and loan rates you want. Just look at the table below, which shows what kind of 30-year fixed mortgage rates different FICO scores qualify you for. So I would spend the time to check yours out and make sure it's as high as you can make it.

Your FICO Score Can Cost or SAVE You Thousands

FICO range	APR
720–850	6.507%
700–719	6.632%
675–699	7.170%
620–674	8.320%
560–619	9.344%
500–559	9.882%

Source: MyFico.com (6/22/02)

STEP NINE
If you are drowning in debt, get help.

Debt problems are the worst. They can cripple your spirit, break your courage, threaten your marriage, and even ruin your health. Fortunately, for those of you who feel overwhelmed, there are places you can turn to for help. Unfortunately, there are also more than a few companies that try to take advantage of people with debt problems. Not a day goes by that my e-mail inbox doesn't fill up with "fix your credit" offers. There are even infomercials on TV that purport to show you how to get out of debt.

As a rule, fraudulent debt-counseling services overpromise and underdeliver.

Here's What Reputable Debt Counselors Can't Do:
- They can't "erase" a bad credit problem.
- They can't get you "out of debt."
- They can't provide a quick fix to your problem.

A debt-counseling or -consolidation service that implies it can do any of the above is lying to you. Chances are it took you years to get into trouble with credit-card debt. And chances are it will take you years to get out of it.

Here's What Reputable Debt Counselors Can Do:
- They can help you figure out how and why you got in debt in the first place.
- They can help you figure out whom you owe and how much.
- They can help you come up with a plan to pay off or consolidate your debts.

Two highly regarded debt-counseling agencies are **Consumer Credit Counseling Services** and **Myvesta.org.**

CCCS is an offshoot of the National Foundation for Credit Counseling, the nation's oldest national nonprofit organization for consumer counseling and education on budgeting, credit, and debt resolution. It has more than 1,300 local affiliates around the nation. You can find one near you by telephoning (toll-free) 800-388-2227 or by going online to www.nfcc.org.

Like CCCS, Myvesta is also a nonprofit agency devoted to helping people solve their credit problems. It specializes in assisting people who owe a *lot* of money. According to cofounder Steve Rhode, the average Myvesta client is on the hook for more than $100,000 in consumer debt. So if you find yourself with tens of thousands of dollars in debt, you may want to check with them first. You can get more information about Myvesta by calling 800-680-3328 or visiting www.myvesta.org.

When you contact one of these agencies, your first goal should be to find out as much as you can about what they can and can't do to help you. One important question to ask is whether using their services will hurt your credit rating. And before you sign on with anyone, check with the local chapter of the Better Business Bureau to see if they have any complaints logged against them.

As always, the key to success is: ***Learn It, Write It, Live It.*** So if you know you need help sorting out your debt problems, make a commitment to yourself to get yourself that help by a specific date, and then write down that date below.

I will get professional help for my debt problems no later than [insert date]

_____.   Signed _____

> ## STEP TEN
> ## If you are in a credit-card hole, stop digging!

I meet people all the time who tell me they have big debt problems—and then turn out to have half a dozen credit cards in their wallet. If you have problems with credit-card debt, you need to stop carrying your credit cards. Why? So you can't use them! When I was a "black belt" shopper, I tried every trick in the book to stop spending money. The only one that worked was to stop carrying my credit cards. Once I had to pay for everything with cash, my spending went way down. Try leaving your cards at home for two weeks and see how your spending changes. I think you'll be pleasantly surprised.

> ## STEP ELEVEN
> ## Stop all those credit-card applications from filling up your mailbox.

Chances are that hardly a week goes by without some new offer for a credit card arriving in the mail. If you have good credit, you could receive as many as one a day. It's mind-boggling how relentless these credit-card companies are. Unfortunately, it's not enough simply to throw these applications in the trash. You've got to shred them first. Otherwise, a thief might get hold of one, apply for the card in your name but with his address, and be off and running with your credit.

The best course is to stop the credit-card companies from mailing you applications in the first place. You can do this by visiting **www.stopjunk.com**, a Web site devoted to helping consumers get their names removed from mailing lists. You should also call the **National Opt-Out Center toll-free at 888-567-8688** and tell them you want to be taken off all of their credit-card mailing lists.

And if you're really serious about getting your name removed from the junk mailers' databases, write to the three major credit bureaus we discussed earlier (Equifax, Experian, and TransUnion) and tell them you do not want to be on any mailing lists for preapproved offers of credit.

> **STEP TWELVE**
> **If you are married or a have a partner,**
> **work on your debt problems together.**

Nothing will ruin a relationship or end a marriage faster than a debt problem that won't go away and keeps getting worse. After I wrote *Smart Couples Finish Rich,* I received countless letters from couples struggling with this issue. To the many people who insist that it's their partner's problem, not theirs, I say you're fooling yourself. From my experience as a financial advisor and coach to couples, I can tell you this without fear of contradiction: You are in this together.

- Although one of you might be creating the problem, it affects both of you.
- One partner's credit problems can ultimately ruin both partners' credit ratings.
- One partner's credit can affect the couple's ability to get a mortgage.

Don't put off dealing with this issue. Run a credit report on both of you today! Then set up a time to get together and discuss how you are doing on this issue. As I say in *Smart Couples Finish Rich,* couples that plan together, stay together.

> **STEP THIRTEEN**
> **Protect yourself from fraud.**

Identity theft and other credit-card scams are becoming increasingly common. Don't think it can't happen to you. To make sure it doesn't, take the following actions the moment the situation warrants.

1. **If your credit cards are lost or stolen, contact the credit-card companies immediately to cancel the cards.** This may seem obvious, but many people put it off for days, hoping the missing cards will show up. Don't wait; most stolen cards are used within hours of being stolen.

2. **If you suspect you are the victim of identity theft, call the federal hot line.** The U.S. Department of Justice now has a toll-free hot line to help people whose identities have been stolen. Call **877-IDTHEFT** and let them know what has happened. The Justice Department will share the information with more than 300 law enforcement agencies throughout the United States and Canada.

3. **If you think someone has found out your Social Security number and is using it fraudulently, call the SSA hot line.** The toll-free number for the Social Security Fraud Hotline is **800-269-0271.** And to minimize the chances of this ever being necessary, make sure your Social Security number is NOT in your wallet, purse, Palm Pilot, day planner, or anywhere else where some unauthorized person could find it.

SAMPLE LETTERS TO HELP YOU TAKE ACTION

LETTER TO CORRECT CREDIT REPORT ERRORS

Before you write a letter to a credit agency informing them of mistakes in your credit report, telephone them and ask exactly where such a letter should be sent. Also ask if there is any particular individual to whom it should be addressed. And when you send the letter, make sure to send it via registered mail.

Date

Name of Credit Agency

Address

RE: Request to correct errors in credit report [insert file number on your credit report] #_____

Dear [insert name] _____:

In reviewing the credit report you sent me on [insert date] _____, I have noticed the following errors.

1. [describe first error—e.g., "You list my date of birth as Jan. 1, 1900."]

This is incorrect. The correct information is: [be very specific here and accompany it with proof if you have it—e.g., "As the enclosed copy of my birth certificate shows, I was actually born on July 25, 1963."].

2. [describe second error—e.g., "You list me as having a charge account with Sears."]

This is incorrect. The correct information is: [be very specific here and accompany it with proof if you have it—e.g., "I closed this account on March 15, 2001. Please note the enclosed copy of the letter I sent Sears instructing them to close the account."].

3. [describe third error—e.g., "You list me as having made two late payments on my Bank of America home mortgage."]

This is incorrect. The correct information is: [be very specific here and accompany it with proof if you have it—e.g., "I have made all my mortgage payments on time. Please note the enclosed copy of my latest mortgage statement as well as a letter from Bank of America confirming this fact."].

Sincerely yours,

[your name]

FOLLOW-UP LETTER TO CORRECT CREDIT REPORT

I noted above that once you inform a credit agency of an error in your report, it has 30 days to respond. Unfortunately, there is a good chance you won't hear from them. You should prepare the following letter to go out via registered mail on the thirty-first day. Try to get the name of a supervisor of the first supervisor to whom you sent the previous letter.

Date
Name of Credit Agency
Address
RE: Second request to correct errors in credit report [insert file number] _____

Dear [insert name] _____ ___:

On [insert date of first letter], I sent you a letter via registered mail requesting you to correct the following errors in my credit report. [insert information listed on first letter]

According to the Fair Credit Reporting Act, you are required to respond to my request within 30 days. For some reason, I have not yet heard from you. Please respond in writing immediately to this second request to correct the above-mentioned errors.

Sincerely yours,
[your name]

LETTER TO CREDITOR DISPUTING MISTAKES

As stated earlier, before you write, call the creditor's customer-service number, tell them you're trying to straighten out an error in your credit records, and ask for the name of the person at the company you should contact. If that's not possible, get the name of the department to which your letter should be addressed.

Date
Name of Credit Card Company or Creditor
Address
RE: [insert summary of dispute—e.g., "Error in my payment record__a/c #"]

Dear [insert name of individual or department]:

I am writing to you today because of an error I found on my credit report. I have enclosed a copy of the report (file #: [insert #] _____), on which I have highlighted the error.

As you will see, the report indicates that [insert brief description of mistake—e.g., "I have an outstanding balance on my account with you of $500."]. This is not accurate. The fact is that [describe actual situation and include proof if you have it—e.g., "As the enclosed copy of my canceled check shows, I paid that bill six months ago."].

I therefore request that you immediately correct your records to show [insert what they should say—e.g., "that my account with you is completely paid up"] and provide a copy of this correction to the following credit agencies: [insert list of agencies you want notified]. Please provide me with written proof that this was handled as soon as possible and in accordance with the Fair Credit Reporting Act (FRCA, Sec. 1681(i)).

Sincerely yours,
[your name]

LETTER TO CREDIT AGENCY CLOSING OPEN ACCOUNTS

Once again, phone ahead to get the name of the person or department to whom
your request should be addressed.

Date
Name of Credit Agency
Address
RE: Request for correction of errors in my credit report (file #: [insert number] _____)

Dear [insert name of individual or department]:

Upon reviewing my credit report (file # [insert number] _____, dated [insert date] _____),
I discovered that it incorrectly lists a number of credit accounts that I had closed as currently being
open. Please be advised that the following accounts of mine are not open and should be reported as
being closed:

1. [insert name of credit-card company and account number]
2.
3.
4.
5.

I have enclosed copies of letters to the credit-card companies again requesting that these accounts
be closed. Please correct your records to show these accounts as closed and provide me with written
proof of same as soon as possible.

Sincerely yours,
[your name]

REQUEST TO CREDIT-CARD COMPANIES TO CLOSE ACCOUNTS

Date
Your Name
Address

Name of Credit-Card Company or Creditor
Address
RE: Immediate cancellation of account[s] [insert a/c number(s) _____]

Dear [insert name of individual or department]:

I recently reviewed my credit report [insert date and file number]. This report indicates that according to your records, my credit account [insert account number] _____ is currently open.

The fact is that I have not used this account since [insert date when you believe you last used the account]. Please be advised that I am not interested in keeping this account open and that I am instructing you herewith to immediately close this account and report its closure to the following credit agencies: [insert agency names]. Please do not call me with offers to retain this account or open any new ones.

Sincerely yours,
[your name]

SOME FINAL THOUGHTS ON DEBT

I've provided these sample letters to make your job easy. But remember the core idea on which this book is built: ***Learn It, Write It, Live It.*** The only thing that will ultimately correct the mistakes you are inevitably going to find on your credit report is your taking action and putting everything I said previously in writing.

So get to work. Make sure to send every letter you write via certified and registered mail. (That way you'll have what the lawyers call a "paper trail"—an indisputable record of you sending your letters and the companies receiving them.) Mark down on your calendar when you need to follow up, and keep a file on your desk with all the relevant information, so you can do so easily with everything at your fingertips.

Of course, all of this takes time, and you can almost count on having to send second and even third letters. But don't get frustrated. Ultimately, this entire process is going to empower you. You are taking charge of your situation, rather than letting others take advantage of you.

Finally, if you are in credit-card debt and you feel helpless, get professional assistance. There is nothing wrong with asking for help. The key with credit-card debt is to recognize that you are ultimately in control and you have the power to do something about your situation.

DON'T WAIT UNTIL YOUR DEBT IS PAID OFF TO START SAVING

The number-one question people ask me is whether they should wait until they have paid off all their debt before they start to save. My answer is "no." I believe that whatever you can put aside each month should be cut in two, with half going to pay down your debt and half being saved for the future (something we'll cover in the following chapters).

The reason for this is very simple. Even if you put every ounce of energy into paying off your debt, it could still take you years to get out of the hole. In the meantime, all of your energy will be going into reducing a "negative," with nothing going into building a "positive." This can be depressing to the point where it can demoralize you.

In contrast, if you can afford to put aside, say, $300 a month and you put $150 of it toward your debt and $150 into savings, you are doing two things at once. You're burying the past while jumping to the future. You'll see progress on getting out of debt and you'll be making financial progress with your savings.

This is bound to motivate you and get you excited about the future. In my experience, money is as much an emotional issue as a numerical one. This approach helps you handle both at once.

Now let's take a look at how to invest for a strong financial future by PAYING YOURSELF FIRST!

PAY YOURSELF FIRST

So are you motivated to save money? Did recognizing The Latte Factor™ change the way you think about saving? Hopefully by now there's been a shift in your thinking and maybe even already in your habits and your actions. Now we are going to look at where you can redirect your Latte Factor so you can start investing for your future. But before we jump right into exactly where you should invest your hard-earned money, let's look at the four basic ways Americans generally get rich.

TO GET RICH IN AMERICA YOU CAN . . .

- Win It
- Marry It
- Inherit It

Or

- *PAY YOURSELF FIRST*

Let's review these approaches.

Win It   You can play the lottery. A lot of people do. Since the first state lottery opened for business in New Hampshire in 1964, more than $465 billion worth of lottery tickets have been sold. My question to you is: Have you won the lottery? Do you know anyone who has? If you do, did they give you any money? I didn't think so. So scratch this alternative.

Marry It This is a real strategy that many people (both men and women) actually try to use. It's been said—and I agree—that if you marry for money, you pay for it for the rest of your life. All things being equal, I'd skip this one, too.

Inherit It There is no question that in America thousands of people inherit millions of dollars from their families every year. But let's face facts. Most of us don't have wealthy parents. And even if you're one of the lucky ones who do, is hanging around waiting for them to die really a financial plan? If hearing your parents say they are feeling great makes you sad—well, that's a little sick, isn't it? So while there's nothing wrong with hoping to inherit money, it shouldn't be something you count on.

This leaves us with only one real way to get rich, and that is . . .

Pay Yourself First

Although most of us have heard about the concept of paying yourself first, there's a lot of confusion as to what it means, particularly when it comes to how much you should save and where it should go. This chapter will clear up the confusion so you can start putting the concept into action.

WHAT "PAY YOURSELF FIRST" MEANS

"Pay yourself first" means just what it says. The next time you earn a dollar, before you pay anyone else any money they may have coming to them—before you pay the government its federal or state tax, before you pay your landlord the rent or your bank the monthly mortgage—you must pay yourself first.

The fact is that most of us pay everyone else before we pay ourselves. The first person we pay is the government through our withholding taxes. Then we usually pay the rent or the mortgage and the rest of our bills. If anything is left at the end of the month, then maybe we pay ourselves by putting a few dollars into a savings or retirement account.

Unfortunately, this approach simply doesn't work. For one thing, by letting the government take its portion first, there's often not enough left over to pay yourself much of anything. Fortunately, there is a way to pay yourself *before* you pay the government, a way where you don't lose a third of your paycheck to taxes. And best of all, it's legal.

It involves using what's called a pretax retirement account. There are many different types of these accounts—e.g., 401(k) plans, 403(b) plans, IRAs, SEP-IRAs, 401(k)/Profit-Sharing Accounts, and Keogh plans and IRAs—and we are going to cover them in detail. But before we get into all of that, let's figure out precisely how much you should pay yourself first and exactly how you should go about doing it.

THE "PAY YOURSELF FIRST" FORMULA FOR WEALTH

To be poor	Save nothing, or spend more than you make every month. (This may seem obvious, but it's worth mentioning since so many of us seem to follow this exact plan.)
To be middle-class	Save 5 to 10 percent of your gross income each month.
To be upper-middle-class	Save 10 to 15 percent of your gross income each month.
To be rich	Save 15 to 20 percent of your gross income each month.
To become super-rich fast	Save 20 percent or more of your gross income each month.

These numbers may affect you in one of two ways. They will either anger you or make you anxious (which may be happening right now), or they can get you excited (which is what I hope they are doing).

If you're getting angry or anxious, let's deal with it immediately. Without thinking about it, write down on the next page your gut feeling about why these numbers are upsetting you.

I'm Upset by Your Formula for Wealth Because:

I can't pay myself as much as I'd like to because . . .

1.

2.

3.

4.

5.

Now think about the following question.

What could you do to change your thinking so instead of getting angry you actually get excited?

For those of you who found my formula for wealth exciting, finish the following sentence.

I'm Excited by Your Formula Because:

I can pay myself first because . . .

1.

2.

3.

4.

5.

INVESTING IS AS MUCH AN EMOTIONAL ISSUE AS A TECHNICAL ISSUE

The reason I had you do this exercise is that investing is as much an emotional issue as it is a technical one. Getting rich really does come down to basic math and formulas like the ones above. The process may seem simple, but it works. Unfortunately, too many of us have all sorts of "reasons" why it won't or can't work for us. The way to defeat this kind of negative thinking is to put those reasons down on paper and then examine them in black and white.

An Easy Way to Start Slowly

The first time I read that you should pay yourself first by saving 10 percent of your gross income, I got angry. Here I was living paycheck to paycheck, often having already spent the next month's paycheck about 10 days before I actually got it.

Then one day it hit me. The only way I was ever going to start paying myself first was simply to DO IT! I was 24 at the time, and that very day I started paying myself 1 percent of my income first. That's right—just 1 percent. Yes, it's a tiny amount, and that was the point. It was an amount I knew I could handle.

Then, after 90 days of not really missing that 1 percent, I bumped it up 1 percent more. I could handle that, too. About a month later, I increased the amount by another 1 percent. Within six months, I was saving about 6 percent of my income, and I didn't notice it. Within a year, I had gradually reached a level where I was paying myself 12 percent of my gross income. Within five years, I reached 20 percent of my income.

I'm not sharing this with you to brag. I'm sharing it because if you're not paying yourself first now, I think I know what's keeping you from getting started, and I can tell you from personal experience that you can change this simply by deciding today to take action. Start by saving just 1 percent if that is all you think you can do, but do it. And remember: If you can work your way up to the point where you are paying yourself 15 percent of your income off the top, you will automatically become wealthy. That's a promise—at that point, it's simply a matter of time and compound interest.

TO BUILD WEALTH, PAY YOURSELF FIRST
AND DO IT EVERY MONTH

Okay, hopefully I've motivated you. Right now write down exactly how much you will pay yourself first.

I, [insert your name] _____, hereby promise that I will begin paying myself *first* _____ percent of my gross monthly income no later than [insert date] _____.

Signed: _____

Cut this out or write it down on a piece of paper and put it by your phone or on your computer so you see it every day.

Now complete the following statements:

I expect my gross monthly earnings to be: $_____

Of this, I will pay myself first the following percentage each month: _____%

By doing this, my monthly savings will total: $_____

In one year, I will have paid myself first: $_____ _____

THE MIRACLE OF COMPOUND INTEREST

When someone once asked Albert Einstein to name the most amazing phenomenon he had ever come across, the great genius replied that it was the power of compound interest. Now that you've written down how much you can save each month, take a look at the table below. It demonstrates the power of saving even a small amount of money each month and then letting it compound. If you do this, you will be on your way to wealth.

Depending on the rate of return, investing just $100 a month and then letting it compound can quickly generate a surprisingly large nest egg.

SAVINGS GROWTH OF $100 DEPOSITED MONTHLY

$100/ month	Interest Rate	5 Years	10 Years	15 Years	20 Years	25 Years	30 Years	35 Years	40 Years
	2.0%	$6,315	$13,294	$21,006	$29,529	$38,947	$49,355	$60,856	$73,566
	3.0	6,481	14,009	22,754	32,912	44,712	58,419	74,342	92,837
	4.0	6,652	14,774	24,691	36,800	51,584	69,636	91,678	118,590
	5.0	6,829	15,593	26,840	41,275	59,799	83,573	114,083	153,238
	6.0	7,012	16,470	29,227	49,435	69,646	100,954	143,183	200,145
	7.0	7,201	17,409	31,881	52,397	81,480	122,709	181,156	264,012
	8.0	7,397	18,417	34,835	59,295	95,737	150,030	230,918	351,428
	9.0	7,599	19,497	38,124	67,290	112,953	184,447	296,385	471,643
	10.0	7,808	20,655	41,792	76,570	133,789	227,933	382,828	637,678
	11.0	8,025	21,899	45,886	87,357	159,058	283,023	497,347	867,896
	12.0	8,249	23,234	50,458	99,915	189,764	352,991	649,527	1,188,242

Now suppose you put your savings into a retirement account such as an IRA or a Roth IRA. The next chart illustrates what can happen if you save just $5.50 a day (or roughly $2,000 a year) and invest it in a retirement plan.

Hopefully, these last two charts got you excited about taking advantage of your Latte Factor™ and paying yourself first.

Now let's roll up our sleeves and take a look at exactly where and how your newfound savings should be invested.

THE TIME VALUE OF MONEY
Invest Now Rather Than Later

BILLY — Investing at Age 14 (10% Annual Return)				SUSAN — Investing at Age 19 (10% Annual Return)				KIM — Investing at Age 27 (10% Annual Return)		
AGE	INVESTMENT	TOTAL VALUE		AGE	INVESTMENT	TOTAL VALUE		AGE	INVESTMENT	TOTAL VALUE
14	$2,000	$2,200	S	19	$2,000	$2,200	S	19	0	0
15	2,000	4,620	E	20	2,000	4,620	E	20	0	0
16	2,000	7,282	E	21	2,000	7,282	E	21	0	0
17	2,000	10,210		22	2,000	10,210		22	0	0
18	2,000	13,431	T	23	2,000	13,431	T	23	0	0
19	0	14,774	H	24	2,000	16,974	H	24	0	0
20	0	16,252		25	2,000	20,871		25	0	0
21	0	17,877	E	26	2,000	25,158	E	26	0	0
22	0	19,665		27	0	27,674		27	$2,000	$2,200
23	0	21,631		28	0	30,442		28	2,000	4,620
24	0	23,794		29	0	33,486		29	2,000	7,282
25	0	26,174	D	30	0	36,834	D	30	2,000	10,210
26	0	28,791		31	0	40,518		31	2,000	13,431
27	0	31,670	I	32	0	44,570	I	32	2,000	16,974
28	0	34,837		33	0	48,027		33	2,000	20,871
29	0	38,321	F	34	0	53,929	F	34	2,000	25,158
30	0	42,153		35	0	59,322		35	2,000	29,874
31	0	46,368	F	36	0	65,256	F	36	2,000	35,072
32	0	51,005		37	0	71,780		37	2,000	40,768
33	0	56,106	E	38	0	78,958	E	38	2,000	47,045
34	0	61,716		39	0	86,854		39	2,000	53,949
35	0	67,888	R	40	0	95,540	R	40	2,000	61,544
36	0	74,676		41	0	105,094		41	2,000	69,899
37	0	82,144		42	0	115,603		42	2,000	79,089
38	0	90,359		43	0	127,163		43	2,000	89,198
39	0	99,394	N	44	0	139,880	N	44	2,000	100,318
40	0	109,334	C	45	0	153,868	C	45	2,000	112,550
41	0	120,267		46	0	169,255		46	2,000	126,005
42	0	132,294	E	47	0	188,180	E	47	2,000	140,805
43	0	145,523		48	0	204,798		48	2,000	157,086
44	0	160,076		49	0	226,278		49	2,000	174,094
45	0	176,083		50	0	247,806		50	2,000	194,694
46	0	193,692		51	0	272,586		51	2,000	216,363
47	0	213,061		52	0	299,845		52	2,000	240,199
48	0	234,367		53	0	329,830		53	2,000	266,419
49	0	257,803		54	0	362,813		54	2,000	295,261
50	0	283,358		55	0	399,094		55	2,000	326,988
51	0	311,942		56	0	439,003		56	2,000	361,886
52	0	343,136		57	0	482,904		57	2,000	400,275
53	0	377,450		58	0	531,194		58	2,000	442,503
54	0	415,195		59	0	584,314		59	2,000	488,953
55	0	456,715		60	0	642,745		60	2,000	540,048
56	0	502,386		61	0	707,020		61	2,000	596,253
57	0	552,625		62	0	777,722		62	2,000	658,078
58	0	607,887		63	0	855,494		63	2,000	726,086
59	0	668,676		64	0	941,043		64	2,000	800,895
60	0	735,543		65	0	1,035,148		65	2,000	883,185
61	0	809,098								
62	0	890,007								
63	0	979,008								
64	0	1,076,909								
65	0	1,184,600								

Total invested = $10,000.
Earnings beyond investment = $1,174,600.

Total invested = $16,000.
Earnings beyond investment = $1,019,148.

Total Investment = $78,000.
Earnings beyond investment = $805,185.

Billy earns $1,174,600

Susan earns $1,019,148

Kim earns $805,185

Billy invested $68,000 less than Kim and has $369,415 more!
START INVESTING EARLY!

THE BASICS OF PAY YOURSELF FIRST

> ### RULE NO. 1
> #### Use a pretax retirement account.

Alert! New Tax Laws

On June 7, 2001, President George W. Bush signed into law a tax-reform bill known as the Economic Growth and Tax Relief Reconciliation Act of 2001. This new law resulted in more than 400 changes in the tax code and greatly improved what you can do to save more money for your future. As confusing as many of these changes may seem, it is crucial that you understand how they can affect you in 2003 and beyond. Please read this section carefully, as you will find that you can now put significantly more money than ever before into tax-deductible and tax-deferred retirement accounts. If you are 50 or over, you can save even more money using the law's new "catch-up" provisions. Happy Savings!

Build Your Retirement Account with FREE MONEY FROM THE GOVERNMENT!

The number-one way to get rich is to keep more of what you make. The best way to do this is to pay yourself first, using what are commonly referred to as pretax retirement accounts. The reason pretax retirement accounts are so popular is that they actually do allow you to pay yourself first before you pay your taxes. Unfortunately, this concept often baffles people—at least until they see the power of it in "black and white." So read and reread this entire section until it feels like second nature to you. When you feel you can explain this section to a friend, you'll know you've got it.

Let's start by looking at why paying yourself first is so powerful.

The Math Behind "Pay Yourself First"

Earn a dollar, save it in a pretax retirement account—and the entire dollar goes to work for you. So if your account happens to earn a 10 percent return that year, at the end of twelve months you'll have $1.10 in savings.

Now let's try saving without a pretax retirement account. Earn a dollar, don't save it in a pretax retirement account—and you pay income taxes on it. If you are a typical taxpayer, you will lose at least 30 cents to taxes. That leaves you with just 70 cents to save. If you earn 10 percent on your 70 cents, at the end of the year you will have 77 cents—and, by the way, the government will probably want a piece of that 7 cents you earned.

So with a pretax retirement account, you have $1.10, while with a regular account you have 77 cents.

Which would you rather have—savings of $1.10 (which will continue to grow tax-deferred) or savings of 77 cents (which will get taxed every single year)? It's so painfully obvious which is better, yet there are millions of people who could invest in pretax retirement accounts at work and for some reason don't do it.

What is really mind-boggling about all this is that the government wants you to save more money. The chart below summarizes the new tax law changes designed to do this.

SUMMARY OF NEW RETIREMENT ACCOUNT PROVISIONS						
Annual Contribution/Deferral Limits						
YEAR	TRADITIONAL & ROTH IRA (UNDER 50)	TRADITIONAL & ROTH IRA (OVER 50)	401(K) & 403(B) PLAN (UNDER 50)	401(K) & 403(B) PLAN (OVER 50)	SIMPLE IRA (UNDER 50)	SIMPLE IRA (OVER 50)
OLD LAW	$2,000	N/A	$10,500	N/A	$6,500	N/A
2002	$3,000	$3,500	$11,000	$12,000	$7,000	$7,500
2003	$3,000	$3,500	$12,000	$14,000	$8,000	$9,000
2004	$3,000	$3,500	$13,000	$16,000	$9,000	$10,500
2005	$4,000	$4,500	$14,000	$18,000	$10,000	$12,000
2006	$4,000	$5,000	$15,000	$20,000	$10,000*	$12,500
2007	$4,000	$5,000	$15,000*	$20,000*	$10,000*	$12,500*
2008	$5,000	$6,000	$15,000*	$20,000*	$10,000*	$12,500*
2009	$5,000*	$6,000	$15,000*	$20,000*	$10,000*	$12,500*
2010	$5,000*	$6,000	$15,000*	$20,000*	$10,000*	$12,500*

*Indexed for inflation

Source: Morgan Stanley

Now that we've summarized the new tax law changes affecting retirement accounts, let's go through them one by one.

THE MOTHER OF ALL RETIREMENT ACCOUNTS: THE 401(K)

The most popular employer-offered retirement program is the 401(k) plan. Nonprofit organizations offer similar programs known as 403(b) plans. The 401(k), which takes its name from the section of the law that brought it into being, is what is known as a self-directed plan. This means that while the plan is administered by the employer, it is directed by the employee. In other words, it's up to you to sign up for the plan and it's up to you to decide how the money you put into it gets invested.

How to Get Started with a 401(k) or 403(b)

The 401(k) and 403(b) plans offer many benefits, but you can't enjoy any of them unless you sign up. That's how you get in the game. Unfortunately, millions of Americans lucky enough to have employers who offer such plans never bother to sign up for them. As a result, they are watching the game, not participating in it. If your employer offers one of these plans and you are not signed up for it, you are missing out on the simplest way I know of to build wealth. So sign up.

When you sign up for a 401(k) or 403(b) plan, you will be asked how much you want to contribute (ordinarily a percentage of your salary) and how you would like your money invested. Your employer will then begin deducting your agreed-upon contribution from your paycheck and depositing it directly into your 401(k) or 403(b) account. In most cases, the process is completely automated and doesn't cost you anything, so once you have signed up, it doesn't take any discipline to keep going.

Once You Sign Up for the 401(k) Plan, You Need to MAX IT OUT!

The second thing to know about your 401(k) plan is that you should MAX IT OUT! That means putting the maximum amount of money into the plan allowed by law each year. Not all plans are equal. How much you can contribute to your plan is based on a complicated formula that involves how many people at your company are using the plan and how much they are investing. The simplest way to find out how much you can put into the plan is to ask your benefits person at work who handles 401(k) administration.

Below is a summary, based on the new tax laws, of how much you can put into these plans in the years ahead.

401(K) AND 403(B) CONTRIBUTION LIMITS		
Year	Maximum Allowable (if age 49 or younger)	Maximum Allowable (if age 50 or older)
2002	$11,000	$12,000
2003	$12,000	$14,000
2004	$13,000	$16,000
2005	$14,000	$18,000
2006	$15,000	$20,000

Note: After 2006, increases will be adjusted for inflation in $500 increments.

Take Advantage of the Free Money Your Employer May Give You

Many employers will supplement your retirement plan contributions with contributions of their own. If you don't already know what your company offers, find out now. Call your benefits officer and get the facts. If you already know what the company offers, make sure you are getting the most out of it. And don't make the mistake of *limiting* your contribution to what your employer may offer. Any contribution from your employer is simply icing on the cake. Your goal is to build a secure financial future and avoid taxes! Read through the following checklist. For any items you can check off now, give yourself a pat on the back. You're on the fast track to a secure future. For any items that you can't check off, do what you need to do to be able to check them off.

_____ *I am making the maximum contribution from my paycheck to my retirement fund.*

_____ *I know what retirement contributions my employer offers, if any.*

_____ *I have taken the necessary steps to make full use of any possible employer contributions.*

If I am not currently maxed out, I will increase my contribution to the maximum allowed by [insert date] _____.

IF YOUR EMPLOYER DOESN'T OFFER A 401(K) PLAN, YOU NEED TO OPEN AN IRA

If a company retirement plan isn't available to you, then you need to provide one for yourself. Fortunately, thanks to recent federal tax laws, it's easier than ever to open an independent retirement account (IRA), and to put more money than ever into it.

Under the Taxpayer Relief Act of 1997, you can open either a traditional IRA or what's known as a Roth IRA. The traditional IRA permits you to contribute pretax dollars (depending on your income and whether you also are contributing to a 401[k] plan); you don't pay any tax on the money until you take it out. With the Roth IRA, you contribute after-tax dollars (that is, earnings on which you are first taxed), but provided you don't touch the money until after you turn 59½, you never have to pay another penny in federal tax, no matter how large your nest egg grows. It's up to you and your accountant to determine whether it's worth more to you to reduce your taxes now by being able to deduct your IRA contributions this year or to save later by not having to pay any taxes on your IRA withdrawals when you retire.

	Traditional IRA	Roth IRA
1. Who is eligible?	Anyone under the age of 70$\frac{1}{2}$ who earns income from a job or is married to someone who earns income from a job.	Same as traditional.
2. How much can I put in?	Because of 2001 tax changes, you can invest a maximum of $3,000 a year in 2002 to $5,000 in 2008. (*See chart on next page.*)	Same as traditional.
3. What are the tax advantages?	Your IRA contributions may be fully tax-deductible, and as long as you leave them in the account, they can grow tax-deferred (including interest earnings and capital gains).	Your money will grow tax-deferred—and provided it has been in the account for at least five years, you can take it out totally tax-free any-time after you turn 59$\frac{1}{2}$. This is a big advantage over the traditional.
4. When can I take my money out?	Once you reach 59$\frac{1}{2}$ (or anytime after that), you can take any or all of your savings. The government will view every withdrawal as income and hold you liable for taxes, unless you contributed after-tax money in the first place. In that case, you're taxed only on earnings in the account. You have to make minimum withdrawals at age 70.	Once you reach 59$\frac{1}{2}$ (or anytime after that), you can take any or all of your savings. Unlike a traditional IRA, you can leave your money in a Roth account as long as you like; you don't have to start making minimum withdrawals at age 70. This is another advantage over a traditional IRA.
5. What if I need my money before I turn 59$\frac{1}{2}$?	Prior to 59$\frac{1}{2}$, in addition to taxes, you may have to pay a 10 percent penalty on any interest or investment earn-ings your initial deposit generated over the years. This penalty doesn't apply if the withdrawal is used (1) for college expenses for self, child, or grandchild; (2) to help finance a first-time home purchase (up to a maximum of $10,000); or (3) to cover health insurance premiums or cover extraordinary medical expenses.	The rules and penalties for early withdrawals here are exactly the same as those for traditional IRAs. The difference is that you won't be paying ordinary income tax to boot.

Under the new tax laws, you can now put more than ever before into a traditional IRA or a Roth IRA. Take a look:

TRADITIONAL AND ROTH IRA CONTRIBUTION LIMITS		
Year	Maximum Allowable (if age 49 or younger)	Maximum Allowable (if age 50 or older)
2002	$3,000	$3,500
2003	$3,000	$3,500
2004	$3,000	$3,500
2005	$4,000	$4,500
2006	$4,000	$4,500
2007	$4,000	$4,500
2008	$5,000	$6,000

Note: After 2008, increases will be adjusted for inflation in $500 increments.

COMPARING ROTH IRAS TO TRADITIONAL IRAS		
	Non-Deductible IRA (balance after taxes)	Roth IRA (tax-free balance)
Annual Investment Rate of Return Tax Rate	$2,000 10% 28%	$2,000 10% 28%
10 Yrs	$30,844.88	$35,062.33
15 Yrs	$58,727.61	$69,899.46
20 Yrs	$101,923.60	$126,005.00
25 Yrs	$169,781.74	$216,363.53
30 Yrs	$277,358.53	$361,866.85
35 Yrs	$448,902.60	$596,253.61
40 Yrs	$723,466.61	$973,703.62

This scenario shows the performance of a non-deductible IRA versus a Roth IRA over 10 to 40 years, assuming 28% tax rate, 10% return, $2,000 annual contribution, and $0 start balance. In some cases, one can deduct a traditional IRA contribution. For the purposes of this example, we assume the contribution was non-deductible.

Source: Research magazine, February 1998

WHAT IF I OWN MY OWN BUSINESS?

If you are in business for yourself, congratulations. The government actually wants you to succeed and become rich. Hard to believe? Read this section and you will be convinced. Being self-employed, you are eligible for the best retirement accounts around. As a business owner, the best way to pay yourself first is by setting up one of the four types of retirement plans meant for self-employed people:

- Simplified Employee Pension Plan (also known as a SEP-IRA)
- 401(k)/Profit-Sharing Plan (brand new for 2002 and beyond)
- Defined Contribution Plan (also known as a Keogh Plan)
- Savings Incentive Match Plan for Employees (known as a SIMPLE IRA)

Under the new tax laws of 2001, you can now save more than ever before in these retirement accounts.

The SEP-IRA (Self-Employed Retirement Account)

This is now by far the easiest of the plans to set up. You can walk into a brokerage firm and set up a SEP-IRA in fifteen minutes. As of 2002, you can now make a tax-deductible contribution of up to 25 percent of your income (to a maximum of $40,000) each year. If you are over the age of 50, you can save even more, and these numbers will be indexed upward for inflation in future years. Because of the new higher maximums, I like SEP-IRAs even better than the old Keogh plans because they require less paperwork and filing with the IRS.

The Amazing New 401(k)/Profit-Sharing Account

The new tax relief act created a powerful new type of 401(k) plan that allows a small business with just one owner-employee to set up a 401(k) plan. What's so amazing about this plan is that it allows you to put up to 100 percent of the first $11,000 in compensation you earn into the 401(k) part of the plan and then on top of that add up to 25 percent of your total compensation for the year to the profit-sharing portion of the plan. Here's why this can be so cool. For example, say your business income for the year is $100,000. Assuming you don't need the cash, you put the first $11,000 you make into your 401(k). Then, at the end of the year, you take 25 percent of your total earnings—in this case, $25,000—and put that into the plan as well. In all, you've put a total of $36,000 into tax-deferred retirement savings.

In 2002, the total amount you save for the year can't exceed $40,000 ($41,000 if you are over the age of 50). Because it's a 401(k) plan as opposed to an IRA, you can borrow from your own plan if you ever need to.

Plans like these used to be impractical because of the high setup fees and administration costs. Today, however, there are a number of companies that can provide 401(k)/Profit-Sharing Plans for as little as $150 a year. They include AIM Funds (www.aimfunds.com), John Hancock Funds (www.jhancock.com), and Pioneer Funds (www.pioneerfunds.com), which calls its plan a UNI-K Plan. If you use a payroll firm like ADP or PayChex, ask them for details, as they are now offering these plans and can set them up quickly for you. These are great plans for a small business where the husband and wife work together, and my feeling is that many more companies will be offering them in the years ahead. Michelle and I established one of these plans in 2002, and it took us only about 20 minutes to set up.

Defined Contribution Plans (Keogh Plans)

For years, there were two types of defined contribution plans: the Money Purchase plan and the Profit-Sharing plan, commonly known as Keogh Plans. To get the full benefits, you usually had to have both and it was, quite frankly, very complicated. If you have one of these plans, it may be time to get it reviewed, as the plans listed above are now equally beneficial if not better and easier to maintain. As I write this, most people I know are closing down their Money Purchase plans and opening profit-sharing plans, SEP-IRAs, or the 401(k)/Profit-Sharing plan I just described above. In 2002, the maximum you can put into one of these plans is $40,000. If you close one of these plans down and switch to a new plan, make sure you file IRS Form 5500 (terminating the plan).

The SIMPLE IRA

Another type of retirement account, called the SIMPLE IRA, provides an easy and affordable retirement program for companies with fewer than 100 employees. The employer contributes a relatively small amount on an employee's behalf (between 1 and 3 percent of the employee's total compensation), while the employee can put in as much as he or she likes up to the maximums shown in the following chart:

SIMPLE IRA CONTRIBUTION LIMITS		
Year	Maximum Contribution (if age 49 or younger)	Maximum Contribution (if age 50 or older)
2002	$7,000	$7,500
2003	$8,000	$9,000
2004	$9,000	$10,500
2005	$10,000	$12,000
2006	$10,500*	$12,500

* For those age 49 or younger, increases after 2005 will be adjusted for inflation in $500 increments. For those age 50 or older, increases after 2006 will be adjusted for inflation in $500 increments.

FIVE-STAR TIP

Many self-employed people put off setting up a retirement account because they are too busy with their business to deal with it. This is a huge mistake. The point of being in business is to build wealth for you and your loved ones. Without a retirement plan, you are passing up a huge tax break and you're not helping yourself to build wealth. Another critical issue to think about when you are self-employed is that your retirement accounts will be protected against creditors in the event your business goes under. So spend an hour, meet with a financial advisor (something we will cover in Step 9), and make sure not only that you've got the best plan for your situation but also that you're funding it correctly.

RULE NO. 2
Make sure your retirement money is invested for growth.

Now let's see where the balance of your retirement money is right now. Assuming you already have some retirement accounts, list on the following chart all the stock and stock-based investments you (and your spouse or partner) currently have. These are your growth investments. (If you're just starting your retirement saving now, go straight to Rule No. 3.)

Stock or stock fund in which your money is invested	Approx. Value
You:	
1.	$
2.	$
3.	$
4.	$
5.	$
Your Spouse:	
1.	$
2.	$
3.	$
4.	$
5.	$
TOTAL GROWTH INVESTMENTS	$

Now do the same for any fixed-income retirement investments, such as money-market accounts, bonds, or bond funds.

Fixed-income assets in which your money is invested	Approx. Value
You:	
1.	$
2.	$
3.	$
4.	$
5.	$
Your Spouse:	
1.	$
2.	$
3.	$
4.	$
5.	$
TOTAL FIXED-INCOME INVESTMENTS	$

Now add the totals for a grand total of your retirement assets.

(a) Growth investments $_____

(b) Fixed-income investments + $_____

(c) **TOTAL RETIREMENT INVESTMENTS** $_____

Finally, let's figure out the percentage of your retirement investments allocated to growth. You can do this by dividing your total growth investments (a) by your total retirement investments (c).

_____ ÷ _____ × 100 = _____%

(a) Growth investments　　*(c) Total investments*

You now know how much you are presently allocating to growth funds in your retirement plan. This is a vital piece of information, but it's only worth what you do with it. I want you to make sure that you've got the very best balance in your retirement investments. Rule No. 3 will show you how to figure out where you *should* be.

RULE NO. 3
Allocate your assets so you maximize return while minimizing risk.

Figuring out the right balance between growth investments and fixed-income investments is known in the investment industry as "determining your asset allocation." Your first step in this process is to decide how much of your money should be put into growth vehicles—stocks and stock-based mutual funds— and how much should be put into safer, slower-growing fixed-income securities—bonds or bond funds.

I use a rule-of-thumb formula to determine the amount of money a particular individual should invest in stocks versus bonds. Do the simple math below:

Start with 100   100
Subtract your age   – _____

TOTAL   _____

The total you just came up with equals the percentage of your assets that you should put into stocks or stock-based mutual funds. In other words, "growth" investments should amount to _____ percent (fill in the number from the "TOTAL" above) of your total retirement portfolio.

Compare this figure to what you actually have in your retirement savings and investments. Are you on track? If not, this is the perfect time to start adjusting your investments so that you are growing your retirement wealth with the most potential and the least risk! While this formula may seem simple, it's actually quite conservative and based on model portfolio theory that works well over time.

If you're just getting started . . .

Most employer-managed retirement plans offer a set menu of investment choices, mainly mutual funds. In Step 8, I'll show you how to research and choose among funds.

FIVE-STAR TIP

Because asset allocation can be complicated, I do recommend that you speak with a qualified financial advisor. I also recommend that you review some of the great information on retirement planning and investing that can be found for free on the Internet. Here are some of my favorite sites:

http://finance.yahoo.com

www.mfea.com

www.financenter.com

www.ibbotson.com

www.nasdaq.com

www.ragingbull.com

www.edgaronline.com

www.quicken.com

www.marketguide.com

www.smartmoney.com

www.quote.com

www.thestreet.com

www.stockselector.com

www.fool.com

www.valueline.com

www.morningstar.com

www.valuestocks.net

RULE NO. 4
Invest in your company's stock, but do your homework!

If your company is publicly traded, one of your 401(k) options may be to invest all or part of your retirement nest egg in your employer's stock. With the demise of Enron and the big declines in the stocks of so many other companies in recent years, there has been a lot said about the perils of investing too much of your retirement money in your company's stock. Even the best companies sometimes stumble, and they can be vulnerable to economic downturns despite an otherwise healthy growth rate.

Many experts recommend that you limit investment in any one company's stock to 10 percent of your total portfolio, whether you work for the company or not. That's a bit conservative for me. If you work for a really great company that you know is well run, I'd consider investing up to 25 percent of your retirement account money (but not a penny more). I used to recommend investing as much as 50 percent in an employer's stock, but in light of Enron and all of the accounting scandals, I think limiting such investments to no more than 25 percent of your portfolio (and to no more than 10 percent for those who are very conservative) is probably more prudent.

The most important thing you should do before investing in your own company's stock is some research. Before you invest, request an "investor's kit," which will include articles about the company, its latest annual report, and its 10-K—a required report filed annually with the Securities and Exchange Commission that details information about the company and its finances. For free information on your company's 10-K (or even their 10-Q, the quarterly financial update), visit **www.sec.gov** and **www.freedgar.com**. For the latest news about your company, a great site to visit regularly is www.cbsmarket-watch.com. If you want to listen to conference calls between company executives and stock market analysts, your company's Web site will probably post them. If you missed a live event, you may find it archived on **www.company-boardroom.com**.

In addition, take advantage of one or more of the many online sites that specialize in providing information about individual stocks (e.g., corporate earnings, industry trends, growth prospects, etc.). The list on page 107 is a good sampling.

> ## RULE NO. 5
> ### Don't borrow from your retirement plan.

I once had a client named Sally who quit her job shortly after filing sexual harassment charges against her boss. The moment she left the company, she received a letter demanding that she remove all her retirement savings from the company's 401(k) plan. (The company had the right to do this, because she was no longer an employee.) This meant that she had to either transfer the money to a personal IRA account or withdraw it in cash—which would mean paying taxes on it and incurring the 10 percent federal penalty!

Normally, this wouldn't have presented a problem. However, a year earlier, Sally had borrowed $15,000 from her 401(k) in order to settle some credit-card debt, and she wasn't yet in a position to pay the loan back. Unfortunately, if she couldn't repay the $15,000 before she left the 401(k) plan, the IRS would consider the loan a premature IRA distribution subject to both taxes and penalties.

Neither a bank nor her parents were prepared or able to give Sally a loan. So she had to pay income tax on the $15,000 she had borrowed, plus a 10 percent penalty—a whopping $7,000 in all! In order to manage it, Sally had to negotiate with the IRS to pay off her liability in installments. All this anguish and expense came about because she had borrowed from her future.

The lesson should be clear. Leave your retirement money alone until you are ready to retire. If you've never borrowed from your retirement account, commit yourself to making that the *last* place you would ever turn. If you've already borrowed and have not yet repaid the loan, use the table below to plan how and when you are going to repay your future!

(a) Total amount I owe my retirement account $_____

(b) Monthly repayment I intend to make $_____

(c) No. of months required to repay loan (a ÷ b) _____

Now you have a plan to get out of debt to yourself (and potentially the IRS). Start this month. The sooner you start paying down your debt, the sooner you'll be back on the right track to a rich future.

> ### RULE NO. 7
> ### Always take your retirement money with you.

When you leave a company where you've been contributing to a 401(k) plan, immediately inform the benefits department that you want to do an IRA rollover. Your former employer will then transfer your retirement funds either to a new custodial IRA that you have set up for yourself at some bank or brokerage firm, or to the 401(k) plan at your new employer.

Why bother doing an IRA rollover when I leave my company?

When you leave money behind in a 401(k) program at a former employer, it's still yours, but your control over that money is far from complete. Say your old company decides to move its plan from one company administrator to another (for example, from Charles Schwab to Fidelity). There's nothing you can do about it, even if you prefer the old administrator. They can do what they want. It's their plan. And when they switch administrators, your account is frozen during the changeover—which means you can't buy or sell any of the holdings in your account. This is exactly what happened at Enron. During one crucial period when the company's stock price was collapsing, the company decided to switch 401(k) administrators—and when many employees rushed to sell the Enron stock they held in their accounts, they found out the hard way that their plan was frozen and they couldn't sell the stock. On the other hand, if you arrange to "roll over" your 401(k) funds into an IRA account in your name when you leave a company, you retain total control over your assets. That's the way you want it. If you have any retirement accounts at former employers, list them below.

Company	Account Name/Number	Amount	Rolled Over (✓)

If you've left any money in retirement accounts at former companies, take action within the next 48 hours to see that it's rolled over into a retirement account at your current employer or into an individual IRA. When you've done that, put a check mark beside that account above.

WHATEVER ELSE YOU DO, TAKE RETIREMENT PLANNING SERIOUSLY

The absolute most important thing you can do to have a major, positive impact on your future financial security is to maximize your contributions to a retirement account and make sure the money works really hard for you. To do any less is, literally, to live beyond your means. Contributing to a retirement plan is not a luxury; it is a necessity! Please give yourself the opportunity to retire when you want with enough money to have all the security—and fun—you deserve.

CREATE A SECURITY PLAN

Now that you've put a solid retirement plan into action, it's time to make sure you are protected against the unexpected.

Let's face it. No matter how well you plan, there are things outside your control that go wrong, and sometimes they go *really* wrong. People lose jobs, spouses, or their health. Businesses go bankrupt. Living situations change. Stuff happens . . . to everyone.

I'm not trying to scare you but rather to make sure you're prepared for a possible "rainy day." Creating a security plan is a lot like making sure that your new car has air bags and seat belts. You're not planning on getting into an accident, but you need to know that if one happens, you'll be protected.

In this chapter, we're going to cover everything you need to do to protect yourself against life's uncertainties. Specifically, we are going to look at what you can do to provide a secure foundation for you and your family that will protect all of you in the event of financial hardship.

SIX ESSENTIAL SAFEGUARDS TO PROTECT YOU AND YOUR FAMILY

Think of these safeguards as the financial seat belts and air bags of your life. You don't have to live in fear of something going wrong; you only have to be prepared, and then get on with the business of living a great life. Put these safeguards to work for you, and you'll free yourself to do just that.

> ### SAFEGUARD NO. 1
> ### Set Aside a Cushion of Cash

HOW MUCH SHOULD I SAVE?

You should always have at least three to 24 months' worth of living expenses saved in case of emergency. Which end of that broad range is right for you depends on your specific circumstances. There are a number of basic factors to consider when figuring out how much *you* need.

1. First of all, think about how long it would take you to find a new job that would pay the same as the job you currently have. If you work in a field or at an income level that makes a new position relatively easy to get, three months' cushion is probably enough. If you think it would take longer to replace your job with another that's financially comparable, then you should have a bigger cushion. During a recession, when lots of people are losing their jobs, you may want to err on the high side, saving even more than you think you should.

2. Now take a look at your typical spending habits. Let's get even more specific. Go back to Step Two and look at what you've recorded about your monthly spending.

How much do you spend each month (that's *total* expenses)? $_____

Now multiply that number by 3. $_____ × 3 = $_____

Your total represents the *smallest* amount of "rainy day" money you should have in a savings account.

3. Next, consider how you feel.

How many months' worth of "cushion" does it take in order to make you feel safe? _____ months.

Multiply that figure by the amount you generally spend each month. The total represents the additional cushion you should have in your security savings.

_____ × $_____ = $_____
(number of months)   *(monthly expenses)*   *(required cushion)*

4. Finally, take the "rainy day" minimum you calculated in No. 2 and add it to the additional cushion you just worked out in No. 3. The result is the total amount of "rainy day" money you need to save.

$\$\underline{\hspace{3cm}}$ + $\$\underline{\hspace{3cm}}$ = $\$\underline{\hspace{3cm}}$
("rainy day" minimum)   (additional cushion)   ("rainy day" total)

It's entirely possible you already have some "rainy day" money put away. The question is whether it's enough. If you're like most people, the answer is probably not.

5. My "rainy day" total from No. 4 above is $\$\underline{\hspace{3cm}}$.

6. My current "rainy day" savings are $\$\underline{\hspace{3cm}}$.

The difference between your goal and your current savings is what we might call your "rainy day" deficit. It's the additional amount you need to save in order to be safe.

$\$\underline{\hspace{2.5cm}}$ − $\$\underline{\hspace{2.5cm}}$ = $\$\underline{\hspace{2.5cm}}$
("rainy day" total)   (current "rainy day" savings)   ("rainy day" deficit)

Covering this deficit should be your security savings goal. Like all goals, in order to be sure of achieving it, you need to Learn It, Write It, Live It. So . . .

My "rainy day" deficit is $\$\underline{\hspace{3cm}}$.

I intend to save $\$\underline{\hspace{3cm}}$ a month to cover this deficit.

At this rate, it will take me $\underline{\hspace{3cm}}$ months to reach my goal.

I intend to start saving toward this goal on [insert date] $\underline{\hspace{3cm}}$.

I intend to reach my goal on [insert date] $\underline{\hspace{3cm}}$.

You've learned it and you've written it down. So now live it.

WHERE SHOULD I PUT THIS "RAINY DAY" MONEY?

Money Market Accounts

The best place to keep your security savings is in what is called a money market account. A money market account is a mutual fund that invests mainly in very secure, very liquid short-term government bonds (and occasionally some corporate bonds as well). Some money market accounts come with check-writing privileges and an ATM card that can also be used as a credit card. The goal of a money market fund is to preserve the value of your deposit and then pay interest. It's the interest they pay that makes these accounts the best place to put your savings, since most regular checking and savings balances earn far less—if they earn any interest at all. As I write this, the going rate for a money market account is about 2.0 percent, but less than a year and a half ago it was 6.5 percent.

So don't let yourself be ripped off by standard bank savings and checking accounts that pay little or no interest. Right now, I want you to stop reading this book and call your bank and ask them how much interest you are currently earning on your savings or checking accounts. Then record the information here:

Name of Bank	Type of Account	Monthly Service Fees	Current Interest Rate
1.			
2.			
3.			
4.			
5.			

Well? What did you find out? Chances are very high that your bank is not paying you any interest on your checking and even charging you for the account. If that's the case, you've got a bad deal and it's time to fix it.

FIVE-STAR TIP

Many institutions that offer money market accounts will lower their minimum-balance requirements if you set up a systematic investment plan (where you automatically put money in the account each month). Ask for details when you speak with them; you may find you can open an account with an initial deposit of as little as $100. Also, make sure to read the account prospectus before you invest. As noted above, money market accounts are mutual funds—which means that while they are generally safe and liquid, they are not typically insured by the government.

Here's a list of some reputable institutions that offer money market accounts. Call their toll-free numbers or go online and check them out. (If you don't have your own computer or Internet connection, try your local library.)

E*TRADE ($1,000 minimum)
(800) ETBANK1
www.etrade.com

Fidelity Investments ($2,500 minimum)
(800) FIDELITY
www.fidelity.com

Merrill Lynch ($2,000 minimum)
(877) 653-4732
www.ml.com

Morgan Stanley ($2,000 minimum)
(800) 688-6896
www.morganstanley.com

Charles Schwab ($5,000 minimum)
(800) 225-8570
www. Schwab.com

Edward Jones ($1,000 minimum)
www.edwardjones.com

ING DIRECT (No minimum)
www.ingdirect.com
(ING DIRECT is aggressively pursuing new investors, so they offer one of the highest-yielding money market accounts in the country with no minimum balance requirement.)

TIAA-CREF ($1,500 minimum)
www.tiaa-cref.com

This list is meant to make it easier for you to find out about money market accounts. It is by no means an exhaustive list, nor am I recommending any particular institution. If you want to do more research into money market accounts, by all means do so. A very fast and simple way to find out more about money market accounts is to get a copy of *The Wall Street Journal, Barron's,* or *Investors Business Daily.* All three of these business periodicals publish lists of the highest-paying money market accounts. Another way to gather information about money market accounts is to go online and visit www.bankrate.com.

You can use the form below to compare what you find out.

Name of Institution	Minimum Initial Deposit	Current Interest Rate

---

SAFEGUARD NO. 2
You Absolutely Must Write a Will or Set Up a Living Trust

If you die without having written a will or set up a living trust, it will be left to the government to figure out what should be done with the money you've saved and the estate you've accumulated. I don't care how patriotic you are—you shouldn't let the government decide what to do with your hard-earned assets. Moreover, if you die without a will, your estate (which is to say all your money and property) will be tied up in probate court, where members of your family may wind up fighting bitterly over who is supposed to get what and swindlers can insinuate that you promised to leave them money. I know you don't want that. That's why you *must* make your wishes known in a form that will stand up to legal scrutiny. The only excuse for doing otherwise is laziness.

The biggest decision you need to make about your estate is whether you should write a will or establish a living trust. Your lawyer can advise you about which would make most sense for you. I usually advise my clients to go with the living trust.

What is a living trust?

A living trust is a legal entity to which you can transfer ownership of any of your assets (your house, your car, your investment accounts, and so forth) while maintaining control of those assets for as long as you live. You do so by making yourself the trustee of your trust. It also enables you to designate who should be given those assets when you die.

The main advantage of a living trust over a simple will is that a properly crafted trust will keep your assets out of probate court, reducing attorney fees and keeping your estate private. Moreover, a living trust can shelter a significant portion of your assets from estate taxes that, in some circumstances, can run as high as 55 percent.

Make sure you work with a qualified attorney or financial advisor to put your living trust to good use. It isn't enough simply to set one up—you need to fund it properly. Among other things, this involves changing the way your assets are legally designated.

The cost of setting up a living trust runs from about $1,000 to $2,500, and it's more than worth it! Here's a quick overview of the five most common trusts available:

THE FIVE MOST COMMON TRUSTS	
Marital and Bypass Trust	• Referred to as an "AB" trust • Mainly used to reduce estate taxes • Enables heirs to inherit potentially twice as much money as a single trust. Check with an attorney for specific details.
Revocable Living Trust	• Designed to protect home and brokerage accounts • Helps your estate avoid probate • Extremely flexible and easy to set up • Can be changed whenever you want throughout your lifetime
Qualified Terminable Interest Property Trust	• Referred to as "QTIP" trust • Often used by wealthy people who've been married more than once • Provides income to your surviving spouse for his or her lifetime • Allows estate to pass to your children or other designated parties on that spouse's death
Charitable Remainder Trust	• Allows you to live off proceeds of your estate after you've donated it to a charity • Donation affords hefty tax advantages • Provides income for you and your children, then reverts to charity after all of you are gone
Irrevocable Insurance Trust	• Protects the real value of your life insurance from estate taxes • Once it is set up, it cannot be changed • Prevents easy access to your policy's cash value

YOUR SECURITY PLANNING INVENTORY:

Yes No

Do you already have a will or a living trust? ❏ ❏

If your answer is yes, great.

If your answer is no, make an appointment with a qualified professional within 48 hours.

If you have a will or trust, was it drawn up within the last five years? ❏ ❏

If your answer is yes, great.

If it has been longer than five years since your will or living trust was drawn up, or if your life has undergone significant changes (in terms of assets, marital status, age or number of children and other dependents, health conditions), make an appointment *this week* with a qualified professional to review and, if necessary, revise your arrangements.

Do your heirs and advisors know where your will or trust is stored? ❏ ❏

If your answer is yes, great.

If your answer is no, get on the phone today to make sure everyone knows.

Have you moved all appropriate assets into your trust? ❏ ❏

If you're not sure, go back and review your trust documents. They should have come with a cover letter suggesting which of your assets you should put in the trust. (If you are a homeowner, did you remember to transfer the title of your home to your trust? This is often overlooked.)

Finally, if either of your parents is still living, do they have a will or living trust? ❏ ❏

If the answer is yes, make sure you know where it is stored.

If the answer is no, make a date now to talk to them about getting things organized.

★ FIVE-STAR TIP

If you feel you can't afford to hire an attorney right now to help you write a will, consider doing it yourself with the help of one of the many will-writing programs available these days online or at computer stores. (This is definitely not as good as having a professional assist you, but it is certainly better than doing nothing.) Visit www.nolopress.com for the leading will-writing software.

SAFEGUARD NO. 3
Buy the Best Health Coverage You Can Afford

Health insurance is not a luxury. It is a necessity. Nothing will wipe you out financially faster than getting sick and not having medical coverage. Even worse, a lack of health insurance could cost you your life. I can't emphasize this enough. The question isn't whether you should have medical coverage; the question is what type of health insurance you should get.

These days there are two basic types of health insurance: Fee-for-Service and Managed Care. I'll describe both below. But before we get into details, here's my down-and-dirty recommendation for medical insurance: Buy the best you can afford.

If you work for a company that offers health coverage, contact your benefits office and review your situation. Chances are your employer offered you a number of choices. Most people tend to choose the cheapest one—HMO coverage (which I'll cover below). All things being equal, that's the opposite of what you should do. Spend the extra $20 to $40 a month and get the most expensive health coverage they offer. When you do this you always get more options and most likely better-quality care.

Your Health Coverage Inventory

	Yes	No
Are you presently covered by a health care policy?	❏	❏

How much per month does your health care coverage cost you? $_____

What would it cost you to upgrade your health care coverage? $_____
    To figure this out, ask the benefits office at work for an updated list of your health care options. Also, read the fine print of your current policy. If anything is unclear, keep asking your employer questions until you're satisfied that you understand. Once you've done this, decide whether the coverage you have meets your needs. Can you afford better? If so, upgrade.

If your employer does not offer you health care coverage, commit yourself to doing the research and taking action *this week* to obtain health care insurance. There are useful resources listed on page 122 ("If You Are Self-Employed").

Review Your Options

As noted above, the two main health insurance options are fee-for-service and managed care. Because managed care tends to be less expensive, it is more popular than fee-for-service. But it may not be right for you. Review the table below—and remember that your needs can change. What's good for you at one time in your life may not be good at another.

Fee-for-Service Plan	• Also known as an indemnity plan • Makes it possible to see your family doctor, whether or not he/she participates in a particular plan • You can switch doctors without having to get permission • You can go to a specialist of your choice • After you pay a deductible ($250 to $2,500), the plan pays for 80 percent of all costs, up to an annual cap • Premiums are high, so few companies offer this kind of coverage
HMO Coverage	• Coverage through a health maintenance organization • Select your doctor from a list of participating physicians • Primary-care physician acts as referral for all specialist needs • Specialists must also be selected from a list of participating physicians • Care outside the program may or may not be approved for payment • Relatively inexpensive, with low copayments
PPO Coverage	• Coverage through a preferred-provider organization • Primary-care physician referral not needed for a specialist • Specialist need not be a participating member of the organization to have at least some of the cost covered • More expensive than HMOs, with slightly higher copayments • May require an annual out-of-pocket deductible of between $250 and $500 before coverage kicks in
POS Coverage	• Coverage through a point-of-service plan • Offers the widest array of choices of any managed-care plan • Allows you to stay within the plan's network of physicians for a cost saving • Allows you to go outside the network for the additional cost of a deductible • Typically the most expensive choice available through an employer, but it provides the most options

Again, my recommendation is to go with the best plan you can afford. After all, this is your health we're talking about.

- **If you're married,** and both of you have company-sponsored plans, review each carefully to see which is better, then figure out if it makes sense to have both of you covered by it. Even if there isn't a cost advantage, there may be a quality advantage.
- **If you are planning to have children,** make sure you've got good maternity coverage. When in doubt, ask for guidance from your health care provider, friends who have children, and your company's benefits department.

If You Are Self-Employed

Self-employment obviously leaves you without company-provided health insurance, unless you're married to someone whose company benefits both include you and suit your needs. But you may still have plenty of options. If you belong to a professional association, you may be eligible for group insurance. You can also talk to an independent insurance professional about getting individual coverage. Or go online to do your own research. Here's a list of information sources to get you started:

AllBusiness
(415) 581-7600
www.allbusiness.com

MasterQuote of America, Inc.
(800) 337-5433
www.masterquote.com

e-Insure Services, Inc.
(312) 663-9663
www.einsurance.com

Quotesmith.com, Inc.
(800) 556-9393
www.quotesmith.com

InsWeb Corp.
(916) 853-3300
www.insweb.com

eHealthInsurance.com
(800) 997-8860
www.ehealthinsurance.com

MAKE SURE YOU KNOW YOUR COBRA RIGHTS

When you leave an employer who has provided you with health benefits, you have a legal right to continue your medical coverage. Under what's known as

COBRA (named for the Consolidated Omnibus Budget Reconciliation Act of 1985, which established this right), you can keep your health coverage for up to 18 months after you leave your job. You have to pay for the coverage yourself, but at least you'll have a policy to protect you while you look for a new job or new health coverage. Keep in mind that when you leave a job, you have only 60 days to notify the insurance carrier that you want to exercise your COBRA rights, so don't let this slip your mind.

SAFEGUARD NO. 4
Protect Those Who Depend on You with Life Insurance

First let me start by sharing some good news you won't hear very often: You may not need life insurance! Life insurance is too often sold to people who don't really require it. So before you start worrying about how much life insurance is going to cost you, let's first figure out if you even need it.

YOU DON'T NEED LIFE INSURANCE IF . . .

- You are young, single, and don't have any dependents
- You are not concerned about leaving money (an estate) to anyone
- You are not planning to have children and you don't know if you will ever get married

YOU DO NEED LIFE INSURANCE IF . . .

- You have dependents
- You are married, owe a lot of money, and want to protect your spouse
- You have people or organizations you want to leave money to
- You have completely maxed out your retirement contributions and are looking for another tax-deferred way to save money.
- You have a large estate and want to use insurance to reduce potential estate taxes

The key to making a smart decision about life insurance is to assess your situation accurately. Figure out if it makes sense for you—and, if so, how much coverage you really need.

Assess Your Situation

	Yes	No
Do you (and/or your spouse) currently have life insurance?	❏	❏

If yes, how much coverage do you have? $_____

How much coverage does your spouse have? $_____

	Yes	No
Do you (and/or your spouse) have an employer-provided life insurance policy?	❏	❏
If yes, is it portable (i.e., would you keep it if you left your job)?	❏	❏

If yes, great!
If no, pull out of that policy and shop for a new one that you
can take with you.

Who depends on your income right now? (List your dependents below.)

1.

2.

3.

4.

5.

A. Estimate what it costs everyone who depends on
you to live for a year. $_____

B. What would it cost, in terms of major debts that
would need to be paid off or expenses that you
might incur (such as funeral costs, estate taxes,
and probate costs), if you were to die tomorrow? + $_____

TOTAL COSTS (A + B) $_____

Experts recommend that your life insurance coverage should total somewhere between 6 and 20 times the "total cost" figure you just calculated (A+B). To help you decide where you want to fall within that range, ask yourself the following:

1. What are my current assets?

2. How much of my debt do I want to be paid off in the event of my death?

3. Do I want to spare my dependents from having to work? If so, how much would it take?

4. Will my spouse/partner need help with child care? If so, in addition to funeral expenses, what would it cost to hire someone to take care of the children?

5. How many years' worth of cushion do I want to provide my dependents?

Ultimately, the decision is up to you and your family. Don't allow someone to "push" you to purchase more insurance than you can afford or feel comfortable buying.

Review Your Options

There are hundreds of different kinds of life-insurance policies. But they all boil down to two basic types:

THE TWO TYPES OF LIFE INSURANCE	
TERM INSURANCE	• You pay a premium • Upon your death, the company pays your beneficiary a death benefit • Relatively inexpensive • Relatively easy to acquire • Builds no cash value • Sole purpose is to provide your beneficiaries with a death benefit
—"Annual Renewable Term"	• Provides a constant death benefit, but the premiums increase each year (good for young people, because it is very inexpensive to start)
—"Level Term"	• Provides constant death benefit *and* premium for the number of years you choose (good for anyone other than those buying life insurance as an investment)
PERMANENT INSURANCE	• Also known as "cash value" insurance • Allows you to combine an insurance policy with forced savings • Relatively expensive • Insurance agents make a lot of money off these policies
—"Whole Life"	• "Cash value" policy with surcharge added to premium that is then invested by insurer for earnings to your account • Investment tends to be so conservative that it earns little
—"Universal Life"	• Similar to "whole life," but invested more aggressively • Can earn at a better rate, but also can lose at a greater rate
—"Variable Universal Life"	• Good if you want a life insurance policy that doubles as a retirement vehicle • "Cash value" policy that allows you to choose how your funds will be invested • Gains are tax-deferred

Should you consider variable universal life insurance?

For most people, I generally recommend term life insurance (level term). However, under some circumstances, variable universal life policy makes sense. To decide which is best for you, ask yourself the following:

		Yes	No
1.	Do you (and/or your spouse) currently have life insurance?	❑	❑
2.	Do you have at least 15 years to invest in the policy?	❑	❑
3.	Do you earn a high income (at least $100,000 a year)?	❑	❑
4.	Are you already maxing out contributions to a qualified retirement plan?	❑	❑
5.	Do you understand the risks associated with mutual funds?	❑	❑

If you answered "yes" to all five questions, you may want to consider variable universal life insurance. Otherwise, stick with level term. And forget variable universal life if you're not already fully utilizing a 401(k) plan, deductible IRA, or other tax-deferred retirement account.

IF YOU BOUGHT YOUR POLICY BEFORE 1997, YOU MAY BE PAYING TOO MUCH!

The good news is that life insurance is significantly less expensive now than ever before. If your current insurance policy is more than five years old, you can probably reduce the cost of insurance by 10 to 50 percent (depending on your health and coverage type). To find an insurance professional who can actually help you—and not just try to sell you all sorts of coverage you don't really need—ask your friends and coworkers for recommendations. Whomever you hire to help you with your insurance needs, make sure they have at least five years of experience.

If you'd rather not buy life insurance through an agent or broker, here are some companies or buying services you can contact directly.

Ameritas
(800) 552-3553
www.ameritas.com

MasterQuote of America, Inc.
(800) 337-5433
www.masterquote.com

e-INSURE Services, Inc.
(312) 663-9663
www.einsurance.com

Quotesmith.com Inc.
(800) 556-9393
www.quotesmith.com

InsWeb Corp.
(916) 853-3300
www.insweb.com

USAA Life Insurance Company
(800) 531-8000
www.usaa.com

SAFEGUARD NO. 5
Protect Yourself and Your Income with Disability Insurance

Here's an unpleasant but inescapable fact: If you don't have insurance to cover long-term disability, you are playing Russian roulette with your income. Here's something to consider. In any given year . . .

- One out of every 106 people will die.
- One out of every 88 homes will catch fire.
- One out of every 70 cars will be involved in a serious accident.

But . . .

One out of every 10 people will have to cope with a severe disability!

The question is not whether you need disability insurance; it is *how much* you need. Let's take another short inventory.

	Yes	No
Do you currently have disability insurance?	❏	❏
If yes, do you pay for it?	❏	❏
Does your employer offer a supplemental disability insurance policy?	❏	❏
If yes, do you know how much extra coverage this policy would provide?	❏	❏

Don't assume that disability is included in your benefits package. First thing tomorrow, telephone your benefits department and find out. If you don't presently have disability coverage, find out if you can add it. If you're self-employed and lack disability insurance, make a point of getting it now.

You need to apply for disability insurance while you are healthy. You won't be able to get it if you already have a disability; nor will you be able to fool the insurance company. Don't think you can lie about your health when you buy your coverage. Not only is that both highly unethical and illegal, it's also virtually impossible to get away with. And once the truth comes out, you'll lose your coverage as well as every cent you've paid in premiums.

QUESTIONS TO ASK WHEN YOU GO SHOPPING FOR DISABILITY INSURANCE

Is the disability plan portable and guaranteed renewable?

You want to be able to take the plan with you if you change jobs. You also want to be sure you don't have to qualify anew every year.

What percentage of my income will the policy provide?

The answer is typically around 60 percent, roughly the equivalent of your after-tax take-home pay. As a rule, if you pay for your disability coverage yourself, any benefits you receive are generally tax-exempt; if your coverage is provided by your employer, the benefits are usually taxed. (Check with your tax advisor to be sure.) To get more coverage, you may need to buy a supplemental policy or pay more for your current policy.

Under what circumstances will the policy pay off?

You want to know whether the policy will cover you if you're no longer able to do the work you currently do (owner-occupation coverage), or if it only pays off if you are unable to work at all (any-occupation coverage). Owner-occupation coverage is more expensive, but absolutely preferred.

How long does it take for the coverage to kick in?

Most policies start paying out within three to six months. If you have a cash cushion that can carry you for longer than that, you can probably reduce your premiums by accepting a longer wait.

How long will the policy cover me?

You want a policy that will cover you at least until you reach 65.

Is the coverage limited to physical disability?
Or are mental and emotional disorders also covered?

Stress is a major cause of disability, yet not all policies will cover stress-related disability. Make sure yours does.

IF YOUR EMPLOYER DOESN'T PROVIDE DISABILITY OR YOU'RE SELF-EMPLOYED

The following are some of the larger firms that offer individual disability coverage:

Aetna U.S. Healthcare
(800) 636-2386
www.aetna.com

Continental General Insurance Company
(402) 397-3200
www.continentalgeneral.com

Guardian
(888) 513-2300
www.guardianbrokerage.com

Mutual of Omaha Insurance Company
(800) 775-6000
www.mutualofomaha.com

Northwestern Mutual Life Insurance Company
(414) 271-1444
www.northwesternmutual.com

State Farm Insurance Companies
(309) 766-2311
www.statefarm.com

Unum Provident
(800)227-8183
www.unumprovident.com

USAA
(800) 531-8000
www.usaa.com

FIVE-STAR TIP

Disability insurance is very expensive. When you see how much it costs, you probably won't want to buy it. Nonetheless, it's absolutely essential, especially if you are
self-employed. Recently, one of my friends read my book and immediately signed
up for disability and supplemental disability coverage. A few months later, she was
in a serious accident that will keep her from working for a year or more. Without
her disability insurance, she would have been financially devastated. Fortunately,
now all she needs to do is focus on getting healthy. My recommendation: Find a
way to pay for this coverage. If anything goes wrong, you'll be glad you did.

SAFEGUARD NO. 6
If You Are in Your Sixties, Consider Long-Term-Care Coverage

The extended family that lives together—or even near each other—is increasingly rare in America. As a result, we can no longer count on family members to
take care of us when we get old. Unfortunately, studies indicate that at least one
out of every three Americans will need some sort of long-term old-age care.
With the cost of long-term residential care running as high as $70,000 a year,
and with Medicare generally covering less than 10 percent of such costs, some
kind of long-term-care (LTC) insurance is increasingly a necessity.

Medicare does cover some long-term-care costs, but only if your hospital stay begins with at least three days in an acute-care facility and your condition is such that you require at least five days a week skilled care or rehabilitation therapy. Even then, Medicare will cover only a portion of your costs and only for 80 days. In any case, Medicare may not be around forever, and Medicaid kicks in only if you're destitute.

If you're in your fifties or younger, you probably don't need to do more than think about this. The time to buy is when you reach your sixties. At that point, you should still be in relatively good health, which means that LTC insurance will cost less than if you were to wait until you reached your seventies or eighties.

WHAT LTC INSURANCE DOES—AND DOESN'T—COVER

- LTC insurance covers care in a nursing home, a residential-care facility, a convalescent facility, an extended-care facility, a community hospice, an adult-care facility, or in some cases, care in your own home.
- LTC coverage will not pay for acute care in a hospital (e.g., for a heart attack or broken hip).

WHAT DETERMINES THE COST

The cost of LTC coverage depends on a number of variables, some of which you can change, some of which you can't.

- Your age
- The level of the care you want
- The amount of coverage ($100 a day, $200 a day, and so forth)
- How long before your policy kicks in
- Your state of health
- How long you want your policy to last, should you need it

Although the average length of stay in a nursing facility is three years, I recommend paying the 10 to 15 percent extra that will give you lifetime coverage. You can reduce cost by requesting a higher deductible on your policy. This means it will take longer to kick in. The good news is that it will never kick *out*. I also recommend that you purchase a comprehensive policy. You're probably relatively healthy now—meaning you can't predict what kind of coverage you may need later on. A comprehensive policy costs more, but it gives you the most options—and that's worth the extra expense.

Also, check with your accountant before you sign up: This type of insurance can be tax-deductible.

QUESTIONS TO ASK BEFORE YOU SIGN UP

What exactly does the policy cover?

There are several different types of LTC coverage. Make sure you can answer this question before you purchase it.

How much will the policy pay out in daily benefits?

Most policies pay between $100 and $300 in daily benefits. The exact amount should be spelled out in the policy.

Will the amount be adjusted for inflation?

The answer should be yes. Ask how the inflation adjustment is calculated and how much you will be paying for this feature.

Does the policy contain a premium waiver or will I still have to pay the premiums after I start receiving benefits?

This waiver means you won't have to keep paying while you're in a nursing facility. Obviously, it's better to have one.

Is there a grace period for late payments?

Make sure there is. Anyone can accidentally miss a payment. You don't need to find out the hard way that you don't have this insurance when you need it.

Are there diseases or injuries that are not covered?

The answer should be no! You can never tell what lies in store, so why take chances?

WHOM YOU SHOULD BUY FROM

Even though LTC insurance is a relatively new product, you should stick with companies that have been in the business for at least 10 years. And make sure your prospective insurer has earned top marks from at least three of the major insurance-company rating services: A. M. Best (908-439-2200), Standard & Poor's (212-488-2000), Moody's Investor Service (212-553-0377), and Fitch Ratings (formerly Duff & Phelps) (312-263-2610).

Below are three major providers and one broker of LTC insurance you can begin researching today:

GE Financial Assurance
(800) 844-6543
www.gefn.com

John Hancock Life Insurance Co.
(800) 800-5523
www.jhancock.com

Continental Casualty
(800)775-1541
www.cna.com

LTCinsurance.com
(401) 732-1879
www.ltcinsurance.com

CONGRATULATIONS!

You've completed both your retirement and your security planning. Now you can move on to the fun part of your financial planning—building a fund for your dreams! With these safeguards in place for your future, you can start thinking seriously about the "good life" you're here to live.

RECAPTURE YOUR DREAMS

A DREAM REMEMBERED: THE GREATEST GIFT OF ALL

Throughout this workbook, I've been referring to the idea that you should Learn It, Write It, Live It. This chapter is a little different. In this chapter, you need to **Remember It, Write It, Live It.** What do I mean by "Remember It"? Think back to Step 3, when you wrote down the five values most important to you. Do you recall what that felt like? What you were actually doing was remembering who you are as a person. You were remembering what I call your "Be Factor"—the person you are and want to be.

This chapter is going to take you on a similar journey. It's about remembering ideas and things that are deep inside of you that have been pushed to the side of your life as you've gotten older. It's time for you to remember your dreams—your dreams of both who you want to be and what you really want to do with your life.

DREAMS DON'T COST AS MUCH AS YOU THINK

If I could give you one gift, it wouldn't be money. It would be the gift of finding out what your dreams are and then coaching you on how to create a plan to make them real. What's amazing about this process is how easy it can be. Most people wildly overestimate how much it will cost—in terms of money and time—to realize their dreams. You may be doing this right now, putting off your dreams in the mistaken belief that you don't yet have enough money and time to get the job done.

Don't Bury Your Dreams in a Place Called "Someday"

I'll let you in on a sad reality. Most people don't live their dreams. Most people put off their dreams for some future time when they think they'll be able to get to them. This time is called "Someday."

Someday is a place of buried dreams, buried lives, and buried treasures. It gets created by the busy everyday realities of life where people tell themselves, "Someday I'll do this" or "Someday I'll be that." And when you ask them exactly when that someday is going to be, they say, "It's when I retire," ". . . when I get married," ". . . when I move to a better neighborhood," ". . . when the kids are grown up and gone," ". . . when my health comes back," ". . . when the bills are paid," ". . . when my promotion comes through," ". . . when I meet the right man or woman." The list of possible "Somedays" goes on and on.

In the next few minutes, you will prove this to yourself, and you will change it.

A HALF HOUR TO SOMETHING MIRACULOUS

This chapter can be read easily in about ten minutes. You can literally blow right through it and head to the next chapter.

DON'T.

Instead, I want to ask respectfully that you set aside a half hour of uninterrupted time to read it, remember it, write it, and then prepare to do it. Give yourself the gift of time to really absorb this chapter and do the exercises. The result will likely be an impact on your life that may seem miraculous.

The reason I say "miraculous" is that when you get back in touch with your dreams, they somehow start to show up in your life. For some of you, this could happen in literally a matter of hours. I can't tell you why it works, but time and time again I've seen this both in my own life and in the lives of people I've coached.

MAKE A WISH . . .

What would it be?

Where would you go? What would you do? Whom would you become?

A long time ago in a place far, far away was a person who used to have a lot of dreams. This person had ideas of what they would do with their life—whom they would meet, the places they would go, the things they would see and do. This person dreamed of the impact they would make on the world and the joy they would experience as they got older.

This person is you! Chances are, this version of you existed when you were young. Remember when you were a kid and people asked you what you wanted to do or be when you got older? I'll bet you had exciting answers. I'll bet you had enthusiasm.

When was the last time you asked a kid about his or her dreams for the future and were told, "Well, what I want to do is find a job I hate, work forty to fifty hours a week, get out of shape and gain weight so I'm tired all the time, have a mediocre relationship with my spouse, and then retire in forty years—and at that point start to have fun"?

Can you imagine a 10-year-old saying that? Of course not! But let's be real. This is exactly what is going on around us every day with the people we see and sometimes know. The trick is not to let it happen to you. So let's go back and find that enthusiastic kid you used to be. Let's locate your dreams and create a plan to make them real. Even if this seems far-fetched right now, let's just try it.

DREAMS GIVE YOU ENERGY AND PASSION

Why are your dreams worth finding again? Very simply, dreams are more than an important part of life—they *are* life. They give you energy and passion. They help you believe in yourself and in a future you can create for yourself. And they give you the courage to act.

This is your opportunity—*right now*—to be young, optimistic, and imaginative again. Dig deep to reconnect with the dreams of your childhood. Or take the brave step of dreaming new dreams based on the person you're in the process of becoming. You have everything it takes to make your dreams come true. But before you can get started, you need to identify your dreams and make them specific.

YOUR DREAM EXERCISE

Here's all there is to this exercise. Find a place where you can think and then sit down and make a list of fifty dreams. On the next page, you'll find space to write them down.

Don't overthink this list. Don't ask yourself whether it's realistic based on who you are or what you do today. Just start writing. Think of what you want to do, the places you want to see, the people you want to meet, who you want to be, the impact you want to make, the things you want to have.

This is your list of dreams. If I could grant them to you today, what would they be? You have a half hour. Ready? Go!

MY LIST OF DREAMS

1. _____
2. _____
3. _____
4. _____
5. _____
6. _____
7. _____
8. _____
9. _____
10. _____
11. _____
12. _____
13. _____
14. _____
15. _____
16. _____
17. _____
18. _____
19. _____
20. _____
21. _____
22. _____
23. _____
24. _____
25. _____

26. _____
27. _____
28. _____
29. _____
30. _____
31. _____
32. _____
33. _____
34. _____
35. _____
36. _____
37. _____
38. _____
39. _____
40. _____
41. _____
42. _____
43. _____
44. _____
45. _____
46. _____
47. _____
48. _____
49. _____
50. _____

So how was it? Did you actually do the exercise? Or did you just read straight through to here? For those of you who read straight through, I want to share my story of what writing down this list of dreams did for me. Hopefully, it will inspire you to go back and do the exercise.

HOW MICHELLE AND I CREATED A DREAM LIST TOGETHER

When my second book, *Smart Couples Finish Rich*, was completed, the publisher sent Michelle and me an advance copy. We were going away on vacation, and Michelle read the book on our flight out. I was incredibly nervous as she read it, wondering if she would like it. When she finished, she closed the book, smiled at me, and said, "Honey, I love you. I'm really proud of you. You wrote a really great book. We oughta try some of this stuff."

At this point, you may be laughing. When I tell this story in seminars, the whole room usually cracks up.

I said, "Michelle, what are you talking about? We totally do all of this stuff."

"Oh, I know," she replied. "But let's *really* do it. In your book, there's a chapter where you talk about writing down five dreams. Let's be overachievers and write down *fifty* dreams. Then we can swap lists and talk about them on the beach."

"You are on!" I said. We each took out a pad of paper and started writing.

Within a half an hour, we each had our list. As Michelle suggested, we swapped them—and I was utterly amazed. For one thing, half the items on our lists was stuff we had never talked about (and we had been together for almost 10 years). Yet we had a lot of overlap. For example, we both had written down that we wanted to start bicycling (something we had never done together), we both wanted to visit Montana, and we both wanted to do and give more to charity.

An hour or two later, while still on the plane, I was flipping through a men's magazine and came across an advertisement promoting a 575-mile bicycle marathon across the state of Montana—seven days of riding to raise money for AIDS research.

I tore out the advertisement and handed it to Michelle. "Look," I told her, "one ad, three dreams."

To make a long story short, we signed up for that AIDS ride, we bought bikes (using money from our "dream account"—something you are about to learn how to create), we trained together for five months, and in August 2001 we made the ride, cycling 575 miles across Montana—raising, in the process, nearly twenty thousand dollars for a worthy cause.

It was a life-changing experience. It stretched us physically and emotionally as a couple, bringing us closer to each other. It also turned us on to a new sport and got us very involved in the movement to support AIDS research.

I share this story with you not to brag but simply to illustrate how within an hour or so of writing down our dreams, they began to come true.

Could all this have happened to us if we hadn't written down our dreams? Maybe. But why wonder. Here's what I can tell you from what I've seen in life: Until you write out your dreams on paper, they are merely wishes. But once you write them down, they become real and the forces of good in the world start showing up to help you.

So if you skipped that dream exercise, maybe you should think about going back and doing it.

MAKING YOUR DREAM PLAN FOR THE YEAR

Now that you have created a list of your top 50 dreams, it's time to draw up a practical plan to make them come true. The DreamSheet™ on page 143 is designed to help you focus in on your top five dreams for the coming year.

In recent years, I've enjoyed the incredible pleasure of having readers of my last two books bring their completed DreamSheets to my seminars so they could share with me their successes. In almost every case, these readers tell me that when they wrote down their top five dreams, at least three of them came to pass within a year.

That's the power of writing down your dreams and then going to work on them. Now it's your turn.

DREAMSHEET™
Designing and Implementing the Fun Factor!

The difference between this Dream Worksheet and the Purpose-Focused Financial Plan is that the Dream Worksheet is meant for you to focus on the "fun" stuff in life. In this exercise, write down the top five things that you want to do with your life that sound like "fun"—things you might not consider realistic but you would really like to do.

To do this, simply follow the six steps below and fill in the worksheet on the following page.

1. List your top five dreams. Remember . . . have fun with this. Be "kid-like," not adult-minded.

2. Make these dreams as specific and measurable as possible.

3. What action can you take in the next 48 hours to get the ball rolling? Remember . . . "I don't know" is not an answer.

4. Whom are you going to share your dream with? No matter how crazy it may sound now, the sooner you share it with someone you love and respect, the sooner that dream is going to feel real.

5. What value will this dream help you realize?

6. What will the dream cost? Even if you don't know the exact cost, make sure you write down an estimate.

DREAMSHEET™

TOP FIVE DREAMS	SPECIFIC, MEASURABLE, PROVABLE	48-HOUR PLAN	WHOM WILL YOU SHARE YOUR DREAMS WITH?	WHAT VALUE DOES IT HELP YOU ACCOMPLISH?	WHAT WILL THE DREAM COST?
Example TRIP TO MAUI	GO TO MAUI DECEMBER 2003 FOR 7 DAYS	CALL TRAVEL AGENT; GET MAUI BROCHURES	HUSBAND BILL AND KIDS	FUN/FAMILY/HEALTH	$3,500
1.					
2.					
3.					
4.					
5.					

FUNDING YOUR DREAMS

Over the remainder of this chapter, I'm going to share with you exactly how to set up what I call a "Dream Account." This is a place to put the money it will take to fund your dreams.

Earlier, I said that you might be surprised by how little money many of your most cherished dreams may cost you. Even more surprising, some may not cost you anything at all. I'm sure by now you realize this is true. Maybe you want to take a cooking class, or learn how to paint, or write a book. Dreams like these may require less than a hundred dollars to realize. But other dreams may take a lot more money—and accumulating that money requires planning. The rest of this chapter is about doing what I call *funding your dream account.*

What If I Don't Have Any Dreams Right Now?

Even if you haven't yet created a specific dream list, you should still open a dream account. Once your dream fund begins to grow, you may be surprised at the dreams that come to the surface. Not only that, you may begin to imagine things you've never thought of before.

WHAT IS A DREAM ACCOUNT?

Think of your dream account as a "basket" into which you will put the money that is going to make it possible for you to fulfill your dreams. The best way to start filling this basket is to decide upon a fixed percentage of your income that you will automatically contribute every month. You've already started funding your retirement by paying yourself first for the future. Now it is time to select a percentage of your income to pay yourself first for your dreams.

I usually recommend that people start by investing about 3 to 5 percent of their *after*-tax income. Obviously, if you have dreams that are particularly expensive, you may want to put more than that into your dream fund every pay period. It's up to you. The more money you put away, the faster your dreams can become a reality.

To make this really simple, here is what I suggest you do:

1. Write down how much you earn each month after taxes. $_____

2. How much will you put into your dream account
each month? $_____

3. Decide where you will invest your dream money
(check off when done).   _____

4. Create a systematic investment plan (check off when done). _____

HOW TO FUND YOUR DREAMS

The form in which you keep your dream money depends on how soon you
want to use it. Your dreams may be the kind that can be funded within a year or
two, or they may require planning and saving for half a lifetime. You simply
need to categorize your dreams according to how long it will take to realize
them. Think in terms of short-term (a dream that can be accomplished within
a year or two, such as a luxury vacation); mid-term (a dream that will take
between two and five years to fulfill, such as a down payment on a house); and
long-term (more than five years, such as the ability to quit your job).

FOR SHORT-TERM DREAMS (LESS THAN TWO YEARS)

List below any of your five most important dreams that you would categorize as
"short-term." Estimate the cost, then figure how much time it would take you to
put aside the money needed. Remember: Your money will be earning money.

My Short-Term Dreams Are:	Approx. Cost	Time Frame
_____	$_____	_____
_____	$_____	_____
_____	$_____	_____
_____	$_____	_____
_____	$_____	_____

Here are three kinds of investments that I consider appropriate for short-term dream accounts. All keep your funds as safe and liquid as possible.

Money Market Accounts	• Mutual fund that invests in short-term securities • Offered by most major brokerage firms, banks, and credit unions • Often include such perks as unlimited check-writing privileges and debit card • Usually requires minimum investment of $500 • 3 percent interest rates not uncommon (for current rates visit www.bankrate.com) • Not federally insured • Among the safest investments • Always immediately liquid
Certificates of Deposit (CDs)	• Bank-issued securities • Promise to pay you a given rate of return over a given period • Minimum deposit ranges from $500 to $100,000 • Mature anywhere from one month to 10 years • 5 percent interest rates typical at this writing • Federally insured up to $100,000 • Penalty applied if you remove funds before maturity (may equal as much as half the interest you were supposed to earn)
Treasury Bills	• Fixed-income securities issued by the federal government • Can be purchased either directly from the Treasury Department or through a bank or brokerage firm • Issued in increments of $10,000 • Mature in one year or less • Pay no interest; instead, they are purchased at a discount and redeemed at full price at maturity (i.e., you pay $9,500 for a T-bill you can redeem in a year for $10,000) • Safest investment you can buy • Exempt from state taxes • No penalty for early redemption, but a small commission

FIVE-STAR TIP

For information on how to buy CDs, try these Web sites:

www.bauerfinancial.com
Bauer lists the highest-paying CDs in the nation and provides links to the home pages of banks that sell them.

www.bankcd.com
Here you can research CDs by rate, maturity, and location.

www.bankrate.com
Another good site that lists CDs by rate and maturity.

www.fdic.gov
The official site of the Federal Deposit Insurance Corporation, this allows you to review the financial health of the institution from which you may be thinking of buying a CD.

Keeping It Simple

The easiest way to fund a short-term dream account is to establish a systematic investment plan to fund a money market account. We covered how to find a good money market account in Step 7. Once you've done that, find out if your employer offers a payroll-deduction plan that will fund your money market account directly out of your paycheck. If your employer doesn't, ask the brokerage firm you work with to set up what is called a "systematic investment account." This is an arrangement under which they will automatically deduct a set amount of money from your checking account each month and move it into your money market account. Instruct the brokerage to make the transfer the day after you receive your paycheck. This way you can take your money and fund your dream account before you have a chance to spend it.

There are many advantages to a systematic investment plan. Among other things, the plan is automated, it works on a regular basis, and it may reduce the amount of money you'll need to get started. As I explained in Step 7, many money market accounts require a $1,000 minimum balance, but if you set up a systematic investment plan, they will let you start with an initial deposit of as little as $100 (that's about $3 a day . . . something your Latte Factor™ should handle easily).

FOR MID-TERM DREAMS (TWO TO FIVE YEARS)

Now list any of your most important dreams that you would categorize as "mid-term." As above, include the approximate cost, then calculate how long you think it will take you to put aside the needed money.

My Mid-Term Dreams Are:	Approx. Cost	Time Frame
_____	$ _____	_____
_____	$ _____	_____
_____	$ _____	_____
_____	$ _____	_____
_____	$ _____	_____

The following table lists three kinds of investments that I consider appropriate for mid-term dream accounts. All take advantage of the extra time you have to give you a slightly higher return. They all involve bonds, which are a little less liquid and a bit more risky than cash equivalents. Bonds are essentially IOUs, which means that when you buy one, you are actually lending money to the issuer. The bond specifies when you will be paid back (maturity date) and how much interest you will earn (usually paid in two installments a year).

You have many choices in the bond category. I suggest you restrict yourself to one of the following three types:

Treasury Notes	• Issued and guaranteed by the U.S. government • Issued in increments of $1,000, $5,000, $10,000, $50,000, $100,000, and $1 million • Come with maturities ranging from two to 10 years • Interest you earn is exempt from state taxes
Corporate Bonds	• Issued by a corporation • Only as secure as the issuing company • Range from "very safe" to "very risky" (see chart on page 150 for rating systems) • The higher the risk, the higher the interest rate, and vice versa • Interest rates range from 5 to 10 percent as of this writing • Should be rated at least "A"
Municipal Bonds	• Issued by local governments • Exempt from both state and federal taxes (good choice for people in high tax brackets) • Should be rated at least "AAA" • Pay lower interest than other bonds • Insured against default

Keep this in mind:

- Most investment-grade bonds are fairly liquid. You don't have to wait until they mature to cash them in.
- Bond prices at any given time depend on the general level of interest rates.
- An easy way to invest in bonds is through a bond fund. Funds are managed by full-time professionals, they allow you to start with a lower initial investment, and they offer an out every month, if you like.
- I recommend bond funds to people with less than $50,000 to invest, individual bonds if you have more than $50,000 to invest.

Know the Rating Before You Buy!

Moody's Investors Service and Standard & Poor's both assign credit ratings to corporate bond issues. Here's how to interpret the grades they give.

RATING/QUALITY	MOODY'S	S&P
Highest grade— Smallest degree of investment risk	Aaa	AAA
High grade— Slightly more risk than highest grade	Aa1 Aa2 Aa3	AA+ AA AA–
Upper medium grade— Interest and principal regarded as safe, but not risk-free	A1 A2 A3	A+ A A–
Medium grade— Adequate security, but susceptible to changing economic conditions	Baa1 Baa2 Baa3	BBB+ BBB BBB–

KEEPING IT SIMPLE

To keep your mid-term dream investment incredibly simple, here is what I would do. Ask your brokerage firm to recommend a short-term bond fund with a solid five- to 10-year track record that invests only in government securities and A-rated corporate bonds. If you'd rather research it yourself, go to www.yahoo/finances and run a screen on mutual funds with the qualifications I just gave you.

FOR LONG-TERM DREAMS (3 TO 10 YEARS)

Finally, list any of your dreams that you would categorize as "long-term." Again, figure the approximate cost and how long it will take you to save that much money.

My Long-Term Dreams Are:	Approx. Cost	Time Frame
_____	$ _____	_____
_____	$ _____	_____
_____	$ _____	_____
_____	$ _____	_____
_____	$ _____	_____

Over the last 50 years or so, no investment vehicle has offered as good a long-term return as common stocks. The risks attached to stocks are greater than those for cash equivalents and bonds, but with a longer time frame you can ride out downturns in the market. For long-term dreams, long-run stocks are the best game in town.

When you purchase a stock, you are buying a piece of a publicly owned company. The size of your piece depends on how many individual shares you purchase. You make money on this investment in two ways: (1) by selling your shares for more than you paid for them; and (2) by collecting dividends paid out by the issuing company.

There are three basic ways to invest in stocks. You can:

- Purchase individual stocks directly
- Buy shares in a mutual fund
- With $100,000 or more to invest, use a managed-money portfolio

For simplicity's sake, I recommend that you focus on mutual funds.

STOCK-BASED MUTUAL FUNDS

There are currently more than 13,000 mutual funds available to American investors. This huge number of choices can make things pretty confusing, which is one of the many reasons why you probably should consider hiring a financial professional to assist you in selecting and building a mutual-fund portfolio.

A mutual fund is an investment company that pools the money of many investors and buys various securities (such as stocks or bonds). Investors who own shares of the mutual fund thus automatically achieve the benefit of a diversified portfolio without having to buy individual investments themselves.

Why investing in mutual funds makes sense

In my opinion, here are the key reasons why you should invest your long-term dream money in mutual funds.

1. **They are easy to invest in.** Many mutual funds today allow you to start a systematic investment program with as little as $50 a month. You can set this up, often at no cost, through a financial advisor or with the mutual-fund company directly.

2. **They offer instant diversification.** Even though you may be putting in as little as $50 a month, you immediately enjoy a stake in a portfolio that could include hundreds of stocks and bonds.

3. **They offer professional money management.** The people who run mutual funds are full-time professionals who bring incredible expertise and experience to the job. This includes professional research and trading execution.

4. **They are liquid and easy to monitor.** Most mutual funds are priced daily and are posted in the newspaper right next to the stock tables. Thus, you can easily find out how your investment is doing—every day, if you want to. And most mutual funds allow you to pull your money out with less than five days' notice.

Getting Started with Index Funds

Index funds invest in a portfolio of stocks designed to mimic the performance of a particular market index, such as the S&P 500 or the Wilshire 5000. Because they include many different stocks, index funds automatically give you a diversified portfolio, which is a good thing. When you invest in an index fund (or any stock-based mutual fund), you are investing in the stock market, which means there is risk involved. So make sure you read the prospectus before you commit your money. Below is a list of some popular index funds you might consider.

S&P 500 INDEX FUNDS

Vanguard Index 500 (symbol: VFINX)
(800) 992-8327
www.vanguard.com
Minimum investment:
    For regular account: $3,000
    For IRA: $1,000
    For systematic investment plan: $100 (after meeting initial minimum)

Dreyfus S&P 500 (symbol: DSPIX)
(800) 782-6620
www.dreyfus.com
Minimum investment:
    For regular account: $2,500
    For IRA: $7,500
    For systematic investment plan: $100

Transamerica Premier Index (symbol: TPIIX)
(800) 89-ASK-US
www.transamericafunds.com
Minimum investment:
    For regular account: $2,500
    For IRA: $250
    For systematic investment plan: $50

WILSHIRE 5000 INDEX FUNDS

Vanguard Total Stock Market (symbol: VTSAX)
(800) 992-8327
www.vanguard.com
Minimum investment:
    For regular account: $3,000
    For IRA: $1,000
    For systematic investment plan: $100 (after meeting initial minimum)

T. Rowe Price Total Equity (symbol: POMIX)
(800) 225-5132
www.troweprice.com
Minimum investment:
    For regular account: $2,500
    For IRA: $1,000
    For systematic investment plan: $50

Morgan Stanley Total Market Index Fund (symbol: TMIBX)
(877) 937-6739
www.msdwadvice.com
Minimum investment:
    For regular account: $1,000
    For IRA: $1,000
    For systematic investment plan: $100 (after meeting initial minimum)

Schwab Total Market Index Fund (symbol: SWTIX)
(800) 225-8570
www.schwab.com
Minimum investment:
    For regular account: $2,500
    For IRA: $1,000
    For systematic investment plan: $100 (after meeting initial minimum)

A NEW ALTERNATIVE: EXCHANGE TRADED FUNDS

Exchange Traded Funds (ETFs) are a new class of index funds that trade like stocks on the American Stock Exchange. In other words, you can buy and sell them during market hours just like you can buy and sell common stock. These funds are incredibly liquid, incredibly tax efficient, and extremely low cost. They are less than half the cost of an index fund and about one-sixth the cost of an actively managed fund. And most of them sell for less than $100 a share.

As of this writing, the most popular ETFs are:

- S&P 500 Index Depositary Receipts (symbol: SPY—known as "Spiders")
- Dow Jones Industrial Average Model New Depositary Shares (symbol: DIA—known as "Diamonds")
- NASDAQ 100 Trust (symbol: QQQ—known as "Cubes")
- S&P MidCap 400 Depositary Receipts (symbol: MDY)

ETFs can be purchased through brokerage firms or online trading companies. For more details, go to www.ishares.com or contact the American Stock Exchange at (800) 843-2639 (or at www.amex.com) and ask for its free brochure on ETFs.

BUILDING YOUR PORTFOLIO AROUND "CORE" FUNDS

Once you've accumulated more than $10,000 in index funds, I would start to build a broader portfolio. I'm a great believer in building a portfolio around what are called "core type" mutual funds. The table on the next page lists five types of funds I would consider when building a mutual fund portfolio. I've listed them in the order of most conservative to most aggressive.

FIVE "CORE" TYPES OF MUTUAL FUNDS	
Large-Capitalization Value Funds	• Invest in companies whose outstanding stock has a total market value of $5 billion or more • Tend to be more secure and established • Usually pay quarterly dividends to shareholders • Manager looks for high-yielding large-cap stocks selling for bargain prices • Often offer consistent returns
Large-Capitalization Growth Funds	• Invest in "growth stocks" • Typically do not pay dividends because profits are reinvested • Include such companies as Microsoft, Oracle, Yahoo, Home Depot, Dell Computers, Intel
Medium-Capitalization Funds	• AKA "mid-caps" • Invest in companies with a market capitalization of $1 to 7 billion • Usually newer enterprises hoping to grow to large-cap size • High potential for great returns • High risk
Small-Capitalization Funds	• Invest in companies with market caps from about $250 to 300 million • Very high risk—best for younger investors • Should be limited to no more than 25 percent of total investments
International or Global Funds	• International invest only in stocks from foreign countries • Global invest in domestic and foreign stocks • Recommend 10 to 15 percent of total investment in these funds

AVERAGE FUND PERFORMANCE For the Period: 12/31/84–3/31/02	
Portfolio Investments	Period's Average Annual Return
Dow Jones 30 Industrial Average (including dividends)	13.28%
S&P 500 Composite Index (including dividends)	11.81%
Mid-Cap Funds Average	14.70%
Small Company Growth Funds Average	14.22%
Growth Mutual Fund Index	12.98%
Growth & Inc. Fund Index	12.76%
International Mutual Fund Index/World Index—USA	11.27%
Global Fund Average/Global Equity	11.22%
Balanced Mutual Fund Index	10.97%
High-Yield Bond Fund Index	7.83%
General Municipal Fund Index/Lehman Bros. Muni	8.51%
General U.S. Gov't Fund Index/U.S. Gov't Long-Term Funds	8.25%
Money Market Fund Average/30-Day Index	5.46%

Source: Wisenberger® and Thomson Financial Co.

LOAD FUNDS VS. NO-LOADS: WHAT'S THE BIG DEAL?

It's not enough that there are more than 13,000 mutual funds in hundreds of investment categories to choose from, but in picking a fund you also have to decide what type of cost structure you want. When it comes to mutual funds, there are two types of cost structures: no-load and load. No-load funds don't charge any commission or fees when you buy or sell them, while load funds usually do. But that's only half of the story.

Just because you don't have to pay a sales commission when you buy or sell a no-load fund doesn't mean it's free. Both no-load and load funds charge what are called asset-management fees (often referred to as 12b-1 fees). As of this writing, the average internal management fee for a no-load fund runs about 1.3 percent a year.

Confused? You should be. It's darn confusing. Here's what I can tell you after having crunched the numbers for more than a decade as a financial planner. When all is said and done, load funds cost investors about half a percent to 1 percent a year more to manage than no-load funds.

Is the extra cost worth it? It can be worth it if your load-fund shares are recommended by an experienced professional financial advisor who will meet with you regularly, become your financial coach, and put in place a financial plan to make your dreams a reality.

If you are willing to spend a significant amount of time monitoring the funds you invest in, you may want to do the research yourself and try to save some money. On the other hand, after the Wall Street carnage of the last few years, you may have found that doing it yourself doesn't work for you. In either case, read Step 9, which discusses how to hire a financial advisor, and after that you'll be better prepared to decide whom you want to turn to for financial coaching.

Whether you go the "do-it-yourself route" or pay for professional advice, use the table below to help you compare the costs of the different load and no-load funds. This table should give you a good idea of the kinds of questions you may want to ask about fees before you invest.

COMPARING MUTUAL FUND COSTS			
Fund Type	**Up-Front Cost**	**Deferred Sales Cost**	**Internal Management Fee** (often referred to as 12b-1 fees)
No Load	None	None	0.50% to 1.50%
A Share Fund	5% cost that drops to zero depending on how much money you invest	None	0.50% to 0.95%
B Share Fund	None	Usually starts at 5% and declines by 1% a year, typically disappearing after year six	1.25% to 1.85%; many B share funds convert to A share funds in the sixth, seventh, or eighth year (lowering the internal management fee)
C Share Fund	None	Typically 1% if you sell within 12 months. After a year, no cost to sell	1.50% to 1.90%
D Share Fund	None	D share funds are really A share funds with the load waived. But they are managed in a wrap account and the advisor charges a 1% fee to manage them	0.50% to 0.95%

MUTUAL FUNDS YOU CAN BUY WITH AS LITTLE AS $50 A MONTH!

To help you get started, here's a list of mutual-fund companies that allow you to invest as little as $50 a month and that provide systematic investment plans. (In other words, you can arrange with them to have a specific amount of money automatically transferred from your checking account each month and used to buy more shares in the fund.) As always, before you invest make sure to read the fund's prospectus. And don't invest until all your questions about risks have been fully answered.

Use this list to help you keep track of your research. Check off each company after you've contacted them and gotten the information you need.

NO-LOAD MUTUAL FUND COMPANIES

American Century
(800) 345-2021
www.americancentury.com
Automatic investment minimum: $50/month

Dreyfus
(800) 782-6620
www.dreyfus.com
Automatic investment minimum: $50/month

Freemont Funds
(800) 548-4539
www.freemontfunds.com
Automatic investment minimum: $50/month

INVESCO Funds
(800) 525-8085
www.invescofunds.com
Automatic investment minimum: $50/month

Scudder Investments
(800) 728-3337
www.scudder.com
Automatic investment minimum: $50/month

Strong Funds
(800) 368-1030
www.estrong.com
Automatic investment minimum: $50/month

T. Rowe Price
(800) 638-5660
www.troweprice.com
Automatic investment minimum: $50/month

LOAD MUTUAL FUND COMPANIES

AIM Funds
(800) 959-4246
www.aimfunds.com
Automatic investment minimum: $50/month

American Funds
(800) 421-0180
www.americanfunds.com
Automatic investment minimum: $50/month

Franklin Templeton Investments
(800) 632-2301
www.franklintempleton.com
Automatic investment minimum: $50/month

Putnam Investments
(800) 225-1581
www.putnaminvestments.com
Automatic investment minimum: $50/month

Van Kampen Funds
www.vankampen.com
(800) 341-2911
Automatic investment minimum: $25/month

FOR REALLY LONG-TERM DREAMS (SEVEN YEARS OR MORE)

There is such a thing as a *really* long-term dream (e.g., a second home, a retirement business). If you have a big idea that you don't expect to be able to fulfill for a decade or more, the way you invest your dream fund should be adjusted appropriately. Here are some suggestions:

Variable Annuities	• Mutual funds wrapped in an insurance policy • Money in the fund grows tax-deferred • No income limitations on who can buy them • You can invest as much as you want • You contribute after-tax money • You can elect to start taking money out at age 59 1/2 • You have to pay for the insurance (fee of about 0.5 to 1 percent of the annuity's asset value) • Includes a guaranteed death benefit (your beneficiaries are guaranteed the amount of your principal investment) • Includes a penalty fee if you sell or take distributions within seven years of the purchase date (make sure the annuity doesn't charge more than 7 percent or occur after seven years from purchase)
Individual Stocks	• You have to choose which stocks to invest in • You do not get automatic diversification
Dividend Reinvestment Program (DRIP program)	• Program to allow you to purchase stocks directly from companies that issue them • Once account is set up, no commissions for reinvesting dividends or systematic buying of additional stocks • Allows a start-up purchase with as little as $10 to $25 a month • Set up by purchasing at least one share of a stock through a full-service or discount brokerage OR • Set up by buying stock directly through the issuing company (direct-purchase program) • Detailed information available from www.dripinvestor.com, www.moneypaper.com, or www.sharebuilder.com

SOME FINAL SUGGESTIONS

Before you invest in a mutual fund or stock, always do your research. In the case of a mutual fund, read the prospectus. In the case of a stock, read the company's financial reports and do your own research on the Internet. Even if you hire a financial advisor (which I will cover in the next step), it still pays to do your own research. If a financial advisor recommends a particular portfolio, you'll feel a lot more comfortable if you spend a few hours online or at the library reviewing his or her recommendations. You may also save yourself from bad advice.

Here are some of my favorite Web sites for researching mutual finds:

WEB SITES WHERE YOU CAN RESEARCH MUTUAL FUNDS ON YOUR OWN

http://finance.yahoo.com
Yahoo makes it easy for you to get the information you need quickly. Try the following as a kind of test drive. Visit this site and click "Mutual Funds." Then click on the mutual fund screener. When it asks you for qualifications, select "short-term bond fund," "top 20% performers," "5 years of performance," "invest with less than $250," and "rank by performance." Bam! In literally seconds, you will have a list of top-notch short-term bond funds that require small initial investments. This is just an example of what you can do.

www.morningstar.com
The creator of the leading mutual-fund rating system, Morningstar is often imitated but rarely equaled. This doesn't make them foolproof, but the Morningstar site is where I would start my research. I particularly like the way Morningstar summarizes its assessment of a fund in easy-to-understand language.

www.valueline.com
This service costs money, and is worth it. Their research is very solid. Most professionals subscribe to Valueline, so if you have a financial advisor, he or she may be willing to print out a particular report you are interested in. You may also be able to get this information at your local library for free.

www.quicken.com
I love Quicken. As I mentioned earlier, I use their software for both my business and my personal bookkeeping. Quicken now also offers great stock and screening tools. Check out the system called QuickRank to look at mutual funds.

www.fundalarm.com

This site is also pretty darn cool. It keeps track of how your fund is doing. For example, let's say the fund manager who is in charge of running your favorite fund decides to retire. As an investor, you'd want to know this. If you've registered with this site, you would. FundAlarm will alert you via e-mail to a variety of important developments regarding your investments. They will also let you know if they think it's time to sell a fund because it is seriously underperforming relative to its peers.

www.finishrich.com

This is our Web site. If you click into the resource area, you find a section called "Do Your Own Research" that has links to all of the sites listed in this book—plus many more I couldn't fit in. If you know of any sites we should add to our list, send the address along to us at info@finishrich.com.

CONGRATULATIONS!

You've identified some of your dreams and have made an excellent start at establishing a plan to fund them.

With all of this information, it is possible that you are feeling somewhat overwhelmed. Maybe you have more questions or would like some one-on-one advice. You may be wondering . . . should I hire a financial advisor? While it is certainly possible to take all of the ideas in this book and implement them yourself, there really isn't anything wrong with asking for help. A good financial advisor can become your personal financial coach, who guides you on your journey to living and finishing rich.

The question, of course, is how you find such a person. How do you find a financial advisor who is a qualified financial coach and not just a "salesperson"?

In Step 9, I will help you investigate, interview, and choose a financial advisor who suits you and your interests.

HOW TO HIRE A FINANCIAL ADVISOR

HOW DO I FIND THE RIGHT FINANCIAL ADVISOR?

Over the last eight chapters, you've learned a lot about managing your finances and planning for a rich future. So if that's true, why would you possibly want or need to hire a professional financial advisor? The answer is simple. Enlisting the help of a financial advisor is not a sign of laziness or weakness or ignorance. To the contrary, it's the smart thing to do.

Think about it. Rich people almost always work with financial professionals. In fact, they usually have teams of attorneys, accountants, and financial planners who help them make sure their money is working hard for them. According to one recent study, nine out of ten people with more than $100,000 to invest prefer to work with a financial advisor. This is something to bear in mind if you are not yet as rich as you want to be.

So consider hiring a financial coach. Not only is he or she bound to make the job of managing your money easier, but if you hire a really great one, you'll probably end up achieving much better results than you could on your own.

The real question, then, is: How do you find a great financial advisor? How do you find someone you can trust—someone professional and experienced who really knows the business and will take the time to get to know you, someone who will always put your best interests first?

What follows are my "10 Golden Rules" for finding this kind of financial advisor. They are based on my years of experience as a financial advisor myself, during which I've met literally thousands of other financial advisors.

So let's get started.

THE 10 GOLDEN RULES FOR HIRING A FINANCIAL PRO

> **RULE NO. 1**
> **Get a referral.**

There is no reason to start your search from scratch. Most likely, you already know someone who has a great financial advisor. You just need to ask.

But whom do you ask and what do you ask them? A logical place to start is with your accountant and/or your attorney. Most likely both will be able to offer you more than one referral. (If possible, ask each for at least three names.) Another great way to get an excellent referral is to ask the wealthiest people you know. They don't have to be close friends. They could be people you respect—your boss, a friend of a friend, etc. The wealthier they are, the better, because the rich tend to have top-notch advisors, and the *really* rich tend to have the best.

Just asking someone if they like their financial advisor, however, is not enough. A casual question will generally get you a casual answer, and unless you press them most people will tell you that they "love" their financial advisor . . . along with their doctor, their hairstylist, their attorney, and whoever else you ask them about.

To get a useful referral, you need to go deeper by asking very specific questions.

When looking for referrals, here are some questions to ask:
- Why do you like your advisor?
- How long have you worked together?
- What specifically have they done for you?
- Did they provide a written financial plan?
- How often do they meet with you?
- Do they call you or do you have to call them?
- How do you pay them?
- Do they provide you with a performance statement that shows how much you earned or lost on a quarterly basis?
- Have you had any problems or complaints?
- How is their customer service?
- Will you be compensated for this referral? (This question should be directed to your accountant, attorney, or any other professional who provides a referral.)

If you don't know any rich people, start your search by talking to friends of yours who seem to be good at making smart financial decisions. Chances are the reason they are doing well is that they have someone who helps them. So ask them whom they work with. And remember to ask the questions listed earlier.

The table below can help you organize your interview schedule. In order to do your search justice, plan on conducting *at least* three interviews.

Name of Person Referring	Recommended Financial Advisor	Advisor's Phone No.	Advisor's Address	Date of Contact	Date & Time of Appt.
1.					
2.					
3.					
4.					
5.					
6.					

> **RULE NO. 2**
> **If you can't get a referral, do your own research.**

Even though I believe a referral is the best way to start your search for a financial advisor, some of you will insist that you don't know *anyone* you can ask. Below is a list of referral services that provide information about financial advisors.

As you identify financial advisors in your locale who look like strong candidates, use the table above to record the basic information you accumulate and get your appointments set up.

The Financial Planning Association

(800) 647-6340

www.fpanet.org

The FPA's Web site allows you to search—by zip code—for an advisor who has qualified as a certified financial planner (CFP).

National Association of Personal Financial Advisors

(800) 366-2732

www.napfa.org

This site allows you to search—also by zip code—for financial planners who operate on a fee-only basis. (More about this on page 171.)

InvestorTree.com, Inc.

(914) 395-3470

www.investortree.com

In addition to providing what it calls a Quick Match service that matches your required qualifications to a professional in your area, Investor Tree also does background checks on the advisors it recommends. Financial advisors pay a small annual fee to be included in this listing service; potential clients (i.e., you) pay nothing to use it.

Certified Financial Planner (CFP)

(800) 282-7526

www.cfp-board.org

The Institute of Certified Financial Planners will provide you with referrals to CFPs in your area if you call them. It also offers what it calls a Financial Planning Resource Kit, a collection of free brochures that will answer most of your questions about the subject.

IF YOU USE THE PHONE BOOK

While some people will tell you it's not a good idea to use the phone book to find an advisor, I think it depends more on *how* you look, rather than where you look. If you are highly motivated to find an advisor quickly, one way to start a search from scratch is to open the phone book and look for a top-level nationally recognized brokerage firm in your community. Examples of such firms include:

- A.G. Edwards
- Charles Schwab
- Edward Jones
- Fidelity
- Merrill Lynch
- Morgan Stanley
- PaineWebber
- Salomon Smith Barney

There may also be a strong regional brokerage firm in your area that you can call. Either way, telephone the firm in advance of visiting it. Ask the receptionist if you can speak with the manager of the office. When the manager comes on, explain your situation and describe the type of advisor you are looking for. Believe me, by now you know more about money than 95 percent of the customers this manager will ever meet. So don't worry about sounding ignorant. You won't.

Tell the manager you are beginning your "advisor search" and that you are looking for someone with at least three years of experience. (You may choose to increase that requirement to five years or even more; that's your call.) This is the surest way to avoid being saddled with a rookie—what's known in the business as a "floor broker."

> ### RULE NO. 3
> ### Use the FinishRich Advisor Questionnaire™.

People often hire financial advisors whom they "like." While it certainly helps to like the person you're working with, it's even more important to make sure they are properly qualified and professional. The best way to find out is to ask really good questions during the interview process.

As a financial advisor, I was interviewed by thousands of potential clients. Very few came to the meeting with a list of prepared questions. In the Appendix, you will find the **FinishRich Advisor Questionnaire**™ (on page 203). It contains the exact questions I would use to interview a prospective financial advisor. Either make a copy of the FinishRich Advisor Questionnaire™, or bring the entire workbook with you to your interview. By using the questionnaire, you should be able to find out everything you need at your first meeting.

The questionnaire includes a **FinishRich Advisor Gradecard**™ (on page 216) on which you can rate the advisor's answers to your questions as well as how you felt about the advisor personally. Later on, you can compare the ratings you've given to the different advisors you've met with.

To get an idea of the type of questions you should ask, take a quick look at the questionnaire. The detailed list should really help you make a smart decision about which financial advisor you should hire.

RULE NO. 4
Go to your first meeting prepared.

A true financial professional will insist that you come to your first meeting prepared with comprehensive information about your finances. The good news for you is that once you've filled out the FinishRich Inventory Planner™ (on page 190), you will be ready to do this. Don't be afraid to show this information to a prospective financial advisor. For one thing, they see this sort of personal financial information all the time. For another, they are required by ethical standards to keep this information confidential.

To ensure that your first meeting is productive, I recommend that you bring copies of the documents listed below:

DOCUMENTS TO BRING TO YOUR MEETING	
Documents	**(✓)**
FinishRich Inventory Planner™	_____
FinishRich Advisor Questionnaire™	_____
Brokerage statements (for all your investments)	_____
Last year's tax returns (state and federal)	_____
Retirement account statements	_____

> **RULE NO. 5**
> **A good financial advisor should be able to explain his or her investment philosophy.**

The FinishRich Advisor Questionnaire™ includes a question that asks the prospective advisor to explain his or her unique process and investment philosophy. A true professional should find this question relatively easy to answer. By contrast, someone who is basically a salesperson—that is, someone who is more interested in selling you investment products than in recommending what is really best for you—will find it a lot more difficult.

A real financial professional has a system. As a rule, real professionals develop over the years a unique method by which they:

- Interview you
- Ask questions
- Organize your financial information
- Design a financial plan
- Create an Investment Policy Statement to put in writing how the money will be managed, and the client's stated goals and risk tolerance
- Explain their fees in writing
- Transfer your assets to their firm
- Manage your money
- Service your account
- Provide written performance reports on your account
- Keep you informed of required changes to your plan

If your prospective advisor is really professional, he or she should have a brochure or other written document that shows you exactly what their process is and how you can expect it to work. The advisor may even have a team of colleagues, each of whom specializes in a different area.

The opposite of this sort of advisor is a salesperson who shows up at your house (as opposed to inviting you to his or her office), asks you how much you have to invest, then suggests an investment. These sorts of people try to woo you with talk of big returns, but once they sell you an investment, you rarely hear back from them.

> **RULE NO. 6**
> **A good financial advisor explains the risk associated with investing.**

During the 1990s, when it looked as if the stock market could only go up, a lot of people—including some financial advisors—seemed to forget the concept of risk. Since then, Wall Street has experienced two terrible years (2000 and 2001), and as I write this, 2002 doesn't look as if it's going to be much better. As a result, attitudes have changed.

The late 1990s and early 2000s had a huge impact on how I feel about investing. I have always been conservative, urging clients to adopt a balanced approach to investing. As a general rule, this means a portfolio that consists of 5 percent cash, 20 to 30 percent government bonds, and 60 to 70 percent stock-based mutual funds. If anything, the bursting of the technology bubble convinced me even more that being a "tortoise-style" investor is better than being a bruised—or slaughtered—jackrabbit.

Still, risk is an inescapable part of investing. The key is to understand how to evaluate it. A good financial advisor usually creates what is called a "risk profile" for new clients. He or she will do this by asking you a series of questions aimed at determining how much risk you are comfortable with. This is an important process, and it is worth repeating every few years, as our comfort with risk changes depending on our age and what is going on in our lives. A prospective advisor who doesn't discuss the concept of risk with you is probably not someone you want to rely on.

> **RULE NO. 7**
> **Decide how you want to pay your advisor.**

How you pay your financial advisor is a lot more complicated these days than it used to be. A few years back, most financial advisors were compensated on a commission basis. That is, your advisor earned a small fee every time he or she bought or sold an investment for you. Today that's only one of several ways advisors can be compensated. The main four ways include:

Commission. This is the traditional mode, in which you pay a commission each time you buy or sell an investment. You may pay the commission directly to the advisor or the advisor may be paid by the company that provides the investment product you select. For instance, if you buy a load mutual fund (discussed on page 157), the mutual fund company will pay the commission to the adviser. Still, even when you don't write the check yourself, you ultimately pay for the commission one way or another—usually in the form of fees that are wrapped into the investment product.

Commission and Fee. Some advisors use a combination structure, in which they are sometimes paid by commission but also charge a set fee based on how much of your money they are managing. For instance, in addition to specific trading commissions, an advisor may charge an annual fee equal to 1 percent of the assets under management. If, for example, they manage $100,000 for you, you'll pay them $1,000 a year for the service (typically in quarterly installments of $250 each).

Fee Based. Fee-based advisors never charge commissions. Rather, they charge a flat fee on assets, as described above. As a rule, these fees are assessed on a sliding scale; the more money being managed, the lower the fee structure. A typical fee structure for fee-based advisors these days ranges from 1% to 2.5%.

Fee Only. Fee-only advisors charge by the hour—that is, for the amount of time they actually spend meeting with you and preparing a financial plan for you. Rates can range from $75 an hour to more than $500 an hour, depending on their level of experience and reputation. Such advisors don't actually manage your money for you. They simply suggest what kind of investments they think you should be making and where; it's up to you to follow up on their recommendations.

Which type of advisor should I hire?

The answer to this question depends on your budget and on your temperament. I suggest that when you question prospective advisors about how they are compensated, you follow up by asking them to explain why they use their particular system as opposed to all the other ways advisors charge. Their answer should tell you a lot about their philosophy and their style of doing business. This should make it easier for you to decide what feels best to you.

> **RULE NO. 8**
> **Check out a prospective advisor's background.**

If you follow only one of these rules, follow this one: NEVER hire a financial advisor without checking out his or her background. The reason this is critical is that there are some advisors out there who are not who they say they are. Being friendly and well-spoken doesn't necessarily mean a prospective advisor actually has the licenses, educational background, and experience he or she may claim to have. Make certain yours does. The best way to verify this is to contact the organizations listed below and double-check a prospective advisor's credentials for accuracy.

National Association of Securities Dealers
(800) 289-9999
www.nasdr.com
The National Association of Securities Dealers is the DMV of financial advisors. Always start here. This site lists just about everything you could ever need to know about a financial advisor, including where they went to school, where they have worked, and if there are any complaints listed.

Certified Financial Planner Board of Standards
(888) 237-6275
www.cfp-board.org
This group sets and enforces the standards advisors must meet in order to call themselves certified financial planners. Its site allows you to check the status of a CFP registered advisor.

North American Securities Administrators Association
www.nasaa.org
Organized in 1919, this organization is devoted to investor protection. Its site is dedicated to helping investors protect themselves against securities fraud and can provide you with additional information on this topic.

National Association of Insurance Commissioners
(816) 842-3600
www.naic.org
This group is an organization of state insurance regulators. Through its online National Insurance Producer Registry (NIPR), you can find infor-

mation on more than 2.5 million insurance agents and brokers, including their licensing status and disciplinary history.

> ### RULE NO. 9
> ### Keep in regular contact with your financial advisor.

Hiring a financial advisor is just the first step. You can't meet with him or her just once and think you've taken care of business. I recommend scheduling review meetings with your advisor much as you would with a dentist. Before you leave your initial appointment, schedule your next meeting no later than six months down the line. At a minimum, you should meet with your advisor twice a year. Some advisors schedule meetings quarterly.

If you currently have a financial advisor and haven't heard from him or her by phone or letter within the last 12 months (statements don't count), then you may have fallen into what we call the "client abyss." Get out quick. Either go in and reacquaint yourself with your advisor, or start interviewing for a new one.

Use the chart below to track your contact with your financial advisor. Write reminders to yourself on your calendar, just as you might to keep track of birthdays or appointments. In a perfect world, your financial advisor will have a system in place for keeping in regular contact. Even so, it can't hurt for you to take the initiative and keep track of the relationship in your calendar, appointment diary, or Palm Pilot.

Date of Contact	Purpose of Contact	Next Contact by . . .

> **RULE NO. 10**
> **Never delegate control of your money.**

This final rule may be the most important advice I can give you. Many people who've done everything right in their search for a financial advisor make one fundamental mistake once their quest has been completed. They assume that hiring someone means they are done with the process—that control over their money can now be delegated to the qualified professional they have found. In fact, nothing could be further from the truth.

Finding your ideal financial advisor—your coach—is just the beginning of the process. When you hire a financial advisor, you don't, in effect, give him or her the keys to your car (i.e., your money) and say, "Okay, drive me wherever you want."

To the contrary, you're the one who has to provide the direction. Your new financial advisor is simply a guide, someone who will sit beside you and offer recommendations as to the best way to get where you want to go. You've told the advisor your goals and dreams (your destination), and now he or she is there to help you read the map (provide investment suggestions). But for all the assistance an advisor provides, ultimately you are behind the wheel. You're the one who says "Yes" or "No" to the advisor's recommendations. You're the one who tells the advisor if he or she can make a trade. You're the one who decides how you want to pay the advisor and if you want to continue to work with him or her year in and year out. It's your money and you are the decision maker. Remember that.

While hiring a financial advisor can make your life easier, it doesn't relieve you of the responsibility of your wealth. Ultimately, when it comes to your money, the more you stay involved in the process the better you will do. If you currently work with an advisor who doesn't feel comfortable with your being involved and doesn't take well to your asking questions, find one who does. A good advisor will both guide you and educate you as you take this journey. A great advisor will encourage you to learn more and become more involved. Great advisors know that the best clients are financially educated clients.

IN CONCLUSION

These 10 rules are meant to make your search for a lifelong financial coach easier. Don't let anything I have said scare you off from searching for one. There are many, many good and ethical professionals out there who can help you with your financial decisions.

Remember, your ultimate goal should be to find someone you can see yourself working with for years, maybe even the rest of your life. So take the hiring process seriously but keep in mind that if you hire someone and it doesn't work out, you are hardly stuck. You can start the process over again and continue your search. It may take a few tries to find the perfect advisor, but I promise you—it will be worth the effort.

It's now time for you to move on your decision. If you have decided that you want professional financial help, make hiring an advisor a priority. Decide today by what date you will start your search.

I will start my search for a financial advisor no later than [insert date] _____.

I will complete my search for an advisor by [insert date] _____.

ADDED BONUS

Visit our Web site at www.finishrich.com and click into the resource center. There you will find an entire section on hiring a financial advisor. We will keep this part of our Web site updated with the latest information to help you find the right advisor.

KEEP A FINISHRICH JOURNAL:
WRITE DOWN WHERE YOU WANT TO GO

Have you ever kept a journal? Usually, at one point or another in our lives, we all have tried writing down our thoughts and dreams in a journal. But have you ever thought about keeping a financial journal? What I mean by this is a simple journal in which you write down what you'd like to see happen in your life financially and you record on a daily basis how you are doing. Most likely, you've never done this. At least not until now. This final chapter is about acquiring the habit of financial journaling. You are going to end this workbook by answering a series of questions designed to get you to think, write, and live what is most important to you from a financial point of view.

Throughout this workbook you've been writing down what you want for your life. Now we're going to use this practice to hone in on what you really want your life to look like a year from now. Over the next several pages, I will ask you a series of questions. In the process of answering them, you will gain incredible clarity about where and how you should be focusing your energies over the next twelve months.

YOU'VE PROBABLY LEARNED MORE THAN YOU REALIZE

I want you to think back over everything you've done as you made your way through this workbook. Remember the values you wrote down as part of Step 3. What mattered most to you? Did you learn something new about yourself? What about the dream list you created in Step 8? When you wrote down your list of dreams, did you find a part of yourself that had been missing?

What about the technical know-how you've acquired? In learning how to build a retirement program, a security plan, and a dream basket, what got you most excited? Did understanding The Latte Factor™ change your thinking about how much money you need to make to live and finish rich?

What about the Seven-Day Financial Challenge™? Did you try it? And if you did, did you come away with new ideas about how you could spend less money on a daily basis by watching the little things? What about the Debt-Free Solution™ in Step 5? Did it motivate you to handle your debt and credit record differently? Have you started DOLPing your way out of credit-card debt? Did you decide after Step 9 that you may be ready to work with a financial coach?

You've covered so much ground in this workbook that you may not realize just how much you've learned or done. The reality is that you've made incredible progress on your financial journey to a new you. To hardwire in what you've learned, it's time to answer the questions below and begin the process of creating your very own FinishRich Journal.

THE FINISHRICH JOURNAL

Get yourself in the right frame of mind to start keeping a financial journal by answering the following questions. Think about your answers before you write them down, but don't overthink them. The point is to be honest and accurate, not to try to impress anyone.

What is the most important thing you learned from this workbook?

Based on what you learned from this workbook, what is the single most important thing you are going to do in the next twelve months? How will your life look and feel different as a result of taking this action?

What did you learn in this workbook that you wish you knew earlier? Is there a loved one you'd like to share this new knowledge with?

If you could accomplish only one financial achievement over the next year, what would it be? How would accomplishing this make you feel?

Whom should you turn to for more coaching on financial planning? When will you start?

What are you going to fund your dream basket for? When will you start your dream account?

How could you make the world a better place over the next year? Whom could you help, and what could you do?

MEASURING HOW FAR YOU'VE COME

Read over the answers you just wrote down. Isn't it amazing how far you've come since you started this workbook? Let's measure your progress.

Back in Step 1, you answered the FinishRich Clarity Question by writing down what you felt was the one thing that would have to happen over the next year for you to feel you've made great financial progress. In other words, you identified what you thought was your number-one goal for the year financially.

Go back to page xiv and reread what you wrote. Is it still your number-one goal? If it is, great. You are now going to make this goal even more specific. If it's not—either because your ideas about what is possible have expanded or because you've come to realize that something else matters more to you now—then it's time to put the new you in writing.

Whichever describes your situation—whether your answer to the Clarity Question is still the same or has changed radically—you can get where you need to go by answering the following question.

★ MY NUMBER-ONE GOAL FOR THE YEAR

What is truly your number-one financial goal for the coming year? (Be as specific as possible. Describe every detail of what you hope to accomplish.)

_____

_____

_____

_____

_____

_____

_____

_____

_____

Now that you know what your goal is, and have written it down, start the process of achieving it by completing the following statements:

This goal is important to me because:

I will know I have reached the goal when:

In the next 48 hours, I will do the following to get moving toward achieving this goal:

I will enlist help in achieving my goal by reaching out to the following people or resources:

You may not realize it, but what you've just done is sketch out your personal plan for success.

BECOME UNSTOPPABLE

The number-one obstacle that could stop you from getting started toward achieving the goal you've just written down is . . . you.

Why would you stop yourself? Well, of course, you wouldn't do it intentionally. But there are emotions inside of us called "doubt," "worry," and "fear." They are a three-headed monster that destroys our dreams. They lie hidden away inside of us and appear just as we're about to act. Because of them, we tell ourselves that we can't get what we want or accomplish what we deserve. They are behind the voice that we sometimes hear, whispering to us, "Who do you think you are, anyway?"

You know what I'm talking about, don't you? It's that tiny little doubter inside our heads who likes to say things like, "Based on my experience, you simply can't achieve this goal because . . ."

To quiet this voice—along with all the real voices that may be raised against your goals (such as skeptical friends, coworkers, and relatives)—you have to have a plan. So how do you come up with a plan to counter doubt, worry, and fear? It's quite simple, really. You acknowledge those feelings. Let's be honest. Not all of your doubts, worries, and fears are crazy. At least some of them are based on realistic concerns. So let's deal with them.

What I want you to do right now is use the next worksheet to list all the reasons your brain can come up with that will prevent you from achieving your number-one goal. If achieving your goal will require help from other people (such as a spouse or coworkers), get them involved. Ask them why you'll never accomplish what you want to do. People love to tell you why things won't work.

But don't just list the obstacles. Once you've got them all on paper, then start thinking about—and writing down—specific strategies you can use to overcome these challenges. Because ultimately that's what doubt, worry, and fear are about. They are based on challenges, things that we perceive can stop us from getting what we want.

This simple technique can instantly turn what you may perceive right now as an obstacle into a solution. That's all there is to it—just write down all the challenges you can think of, followed by all the specific strategies you can use to overcome them. It really does work. Try it and you'll see.

A PERSONAL PLAN FOR SUCCESS:
DESIGNING A SPECIFIC PLAN TO OVERCOME YOUR CHALLENGES

STARTING LINE

SPECIFIC GOAL

Date: 2002

Barbara's number-one goal is to retire at age 58 with $1 million.

Current retirement assets are $250,000.

Challenges You May Face	Specific Strategies to Overcome Challenges
Not saving enough money	Maximize contributions starting tomorrow in company-sponsored 401(k) plan
Spending too much money	Spend cash only
Too much credit-card debt	Cut up credit cards; stop using them; make goal to pay off credit cards, starting with smallest debt first
Not making enough money	Look for specific ways at work to "add more value"; meet with boss, discuss strategy to get a raise
Family spends too much money	Discuss specific financial goals and get their input on ways we can work as a team
College costs	Explain financial goals and challenges of retirement to son, Tom, and explain the importance of Tom's getting a job now to help with college costs
Not enough time to get everything done	Wake up an hour early each day and focus on goals and plans

VICTORY

DESIRED OUTCOME

Desired Date: 2010

Barbara wants to live a worry-free retirement that includes travel and lots of fun.

Based on her expenses, $1 million will provide her with an income she cannot outlive.

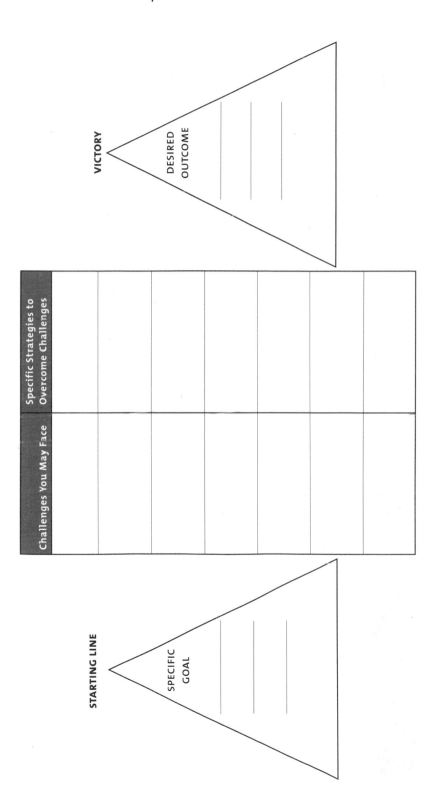

A PERSONAL PLAN FOR SUCCESS:
DESIGNING A SPECIFIC PLAN TO OVERCOME YOUR CHALLENGES

VICTORY

DESIRED OUTCOME

Challenges You May Face	Specific Strategies to Overcome Challenges

STARTING LINE

SPECIFIC GOAL

A SEVEN-DAY ACTION PLAN

This is your final exercise. I want you to write down one thing you can do each day for the next seven days to bring you closer to achieving your number-one goal. Please take whatever you write here and transfer it to whatever calendar system you happen to use.

Day One:

Day Two:

Day Three:

Day Four:

Day Five:

Day Six:

Day Seven:

YOU ARE ON YOUR WAY

Having written down your number-one goal for the year so specifically, along with your personal plan for success and your seven-day action plan, you are seriously on your way. You've committed in writing to what you want and set out to learn how to get there.

A great way to keep motivated is to continue journaling on a daily basis. Get yourself a notebook and each day write down one thing you did right financially. Keep track of your progress. Catch yourself doing well. Reward yourself for every advance you make, no matter how small it may seem.

As we come to the end of this workbook, I again want to say thank you for allowing me the privilege of being your financial coach throughout these pages. I hope this workbook has helped you to get closer to understanding yourself and achieving your dreams. I hope you've learned that much of what you want might not even require money. It might simply require learning it, writing it, and living it.

If you achieve a big dream or a big success as a result of using the tools in this workbook (or any of my other books), I would love to hear about it. Please e-mail me at success@finishrich.com. I promise you I will read your message.

Finally, remember that this journey we call life is an incredible gift. The time to enjoy yours is now. Take time to smell the roses. *Until we meet again along the journey . . . have fun and live rich!*

THE FINISHRICH INVENTORY PLANNER™

Determining Your Net Worth

STEP ONE: FAMILY INFORMATION

Name _____ Date of Birth _____ Age _____

Spouse's Name _____ Date of Birth _____ Age _____

Mailing Address _____

City _____ State _____ Zip Code _____

Home Phone# _____

Work Phone# _____ Fax # _____

Spouse's Work # _____ Spouse's Fax # _____

E-mail _____ Spouse's E-mail _____

SS# _____ Spouse's SS# _____

Employer _____ Job Title _____

Spouse's Employer _____ Job Title _____

Are You Retired? ❏ Yes Date Retired _____ ❏ No Planned Retirement Date _____

Is Your Spouse Retired? ❏ Yes Date Retired _____ ❏ No Planned Retirement Date _____

Marital Status: ❏ Single ❏ Married ❏ Divorced ❏ Separated ❏ Widowed

Children

Name	Phone #	Date of Birth	SS#
1.			
2.			
3.			
4.			
5.			

Dependents

Do You Have Any Family Members Who Are Financially Dependent Upon You or Could Be in the Future? (i.e., Parents, Grandparents, Adult Children, etc.)   ❏ Yes   ❏ No

Name	Phone #	Age	Relationship
1.			
2.			
3.			
4.			
5.			

STEP TWO: PERSONAL INVESTMENTS
(do not include retirement accounts here)

Cash Reserves

List Amount in Banks, Savings & Loans, and Credit Unions

Name of Bank Institution	Type of Account	Current Balance	Interest Rate
Example: Bank of America	*Checking/Savings/Money Market*	*$10,000.00*	*2%*
1.			
2.			
3.			
4.			
5.			

TOTAL CASH RESERVES $ _____

Fixed Income

List Fixed Income Investments	Dollar Amount	Current %	Maturity Date
Example: CD, Treasury Bills, Notes, Bonds, Tax-Free Bonds, Series EE Savings Bonds			
1.			
2.			
3.			
4.			
5.			

TOTAL FIXED INCOME $ _____

Stocks

Name of Company	Number of Shares	Price Purchased	Approximate Market Value	Date Purchased
1.				
2.				
3.				
4.				
5.				

Do You Have Stock Certificates in a Security Deposit Box?　❑ Yes　❑ No

Name of Bank _____　Address _____　Phone # _____

TOTAL STOCKS $ _____

Mutual Funds and/or Brokerage Accounts

Name of Brokerage Firm/ Mutual Fund	Number of Shares	Cost Basis	Approximate Market Value	Date Purchased
1.				
2.				
3.				
4.				
5.				

TOTAL MUTUAL FUNDS AND/OR BROKERAGE ACCOUNTS $ _____

Annuities

Company	Annuitant/ Owner	Interest Rate	Approximate Market Value	Date Purchased
1.				
2.				
3.				

TOTAL ANNUITIES $ _____

Personal Loans
(made by you)

Name	Relationship	Phone #	Total Outstanding	When Due?
1. _____	_____	_____	_____	_____
2. _____	_____	_____	_____	_____
3. _____	_____	_____	_____	_____

TOTAL PERSONAL LOANS $ _____

Other Assets
(e.g., Business Ownership, etc.)

Approximate Market Value

1. _____	_____
2. _____	_____
3. _____	_____

TOTAL OTHER ASSETS $ _____

STEP THREE: RETIREMENT ACCOUNTS

Employer-Sponsored Retirement Plan

Are You Participating in an Employer-Sponsored Retirement Plan? These Include Tax-Deferred Retirement Plans Such As 401(k) Plans, 403 (b) Plans, and 457 Plans. ❏ Yes ❏ No

Name of Company Where Your Money Is	Type of Plan	Approximate Value	% You Contribute
You:			
1.			
2.			
3.			
Spouse:			
1.			
2.			
3.			

Do You Have Money Sitting in a Company Plan You No Longer Work For?

❏ Yes ❏ No Balance _____ When Did You Leave the Company? _____

Spouse:

❏ Yes ❏ No Balance _____ When Did He/She Leave the Company? _____

Self-Directed Retirement Plan

Are You Participating in a Retirement Plan? These include IRAs, Roth IRAs, SEP-IRAs, SAR-SEP IRAs, and SIMPLE PLANS.

Name of Company Where Your Money Is	Type of Plan	Approximate Value

You:

1. _____ _____ _____

2. _____ _____ _____

3. _____ _____ _____

4. _____ _____ _____

5. _____ _____ _____

Spouse:

1. _____ _____ _____

2. _____ _____ _____

3. _____ _____ _____

4. _____ _____ _____

5. _____ _____ _____

TOTAL RETIREMENT ACCOUNTS $ _____

STEP FOUR: REAL ESTATE

Do You Rent or Own Your Home?

❏ Own   Monthly Mortgage Is _____

❏ Rent   Monthly Rent Is _____

Approximate Value
of Primary Home $ _____

−   Mortgage Balance $ _____

=   Equity in Home $ _____

Length of Loan _____

Interest Rate of Loan _____   Is Loan Fixed or Variable? _____

Do You Own a Second Home? _____

Approximate Value
of Second Home $ _____

−   Mortgage Balance $ _____

=   Equity in Home $ _____

Length of Loan _____

Interest Rate of Loan _____   Is Loan Fixed or Variable? _____

Any Other Real Estate Owned? _____

Approximate Value $ _____

−   Mortgage Balance $ _____

=   Equity in Home $ _____

Length of Loan _____

Interest Rate of Loan _____   Is Loan Fixed or Variable? _____

TOTAL EQUITY IN REAL ESTATE $ _____

STEP FIVE: LIABILITIES
(do not include mortgages here)

Credit-Card Debt
(copy details from page 61)

Name of Card/Company	Phone #	Interest Rate	Current Balance
1.			
2.			
3.			
4.			
5.			
6.			
7.			
8.			

TOTAL CREDIT-CARD BALANCES $ _____

Student Loans

School/University or Other Lender	Phone #	Interest Rate	Balance Owed
1.			
2.			
3.			

TOTAL STUDENT LOAN BALANCES $ _____

Personal Loans
(from a bank or individual)

Name/Institution	Phone #	Interest Rate	Balance Owed	Date Due
1.				
2.				
3.				

TOTAL PERSONAL LOAN BALANCES $ _____

Car/Boat Loans

Vehicle	Lender/Institution	Phone #	Interest Rate	Term	Balance Owed
1.					
2.					
3.					
4.					

TOTAL CAR/BOAT LOAN BALANCES $ _____

All Other Debt
(i.e. IRS, Major Unpaid or Overdue Bills, Outstanding Contracts, etc.)

Company/Expense	Date Due	Interest or Penalties	Balance Owed
Example: Acme Construction/bath renovation	*12/03*	*n/a*	*$5,000*
1.			
2.			
3.			

TOTAL ALL OTHER DEBT BALANCES $ _____

STEP SIX: ESTATE PLANNING

Do You Have a Will or Living Trust in Place? ❑ Yes ❑ No

Date It Was Last Reviewed? _____

Who Helped You Create It? (Attorney Name) _____

Address _____

Phone Number _____ Fax _____

Is Your Home Held in the Trust or Is It Held in Joint or Community Property? _____

Risk Management/Insurance

Do You Have a Protection Plan In Place for Your Family? ❑ Yes ❑ No

Life Insurance Company	Type of Insurance (e.g., Whole Life, Term, Variable, etc.)	Death Benefit	Cash Value	Annual Premium
1.				
2.				
3.				

Tax Planning

Do You Have Your Taxes Professionally Prepared? ❑ Yes ❑ No

Name of Accountant/CPA _____

Address _____

Phone Number _____ Fax _____

What Was Your Last Year's Taxable Income? _____

Estimated Tax Bracket? _____

STEP SEVEN: CASH FLOW

Income

Your Estimated Monthly Income _____   Estimated Annual Income _____

Spouse's Estimated Monthly Income _____   Estimated Annual Income _____

Rental Property Income: Monthly _____   Annually _____

Other Income (Partnerships, Social Security, Pension, Dividend Checks, etc.)

Type of Income	Monthly	Annually
1. _____	_____	_____
2. _____	_____	_____
3. _____	_____	_____

Expenses

Use the "Where Does Your Money *Really* Go" form to Figure Your Estimates (see page 19)

Monthly Estimated Expenses $ _____   Annual Estimated Expenses $ _____

STEP EIGHT: NET CASH FLOW

What Do You Earn a Month, After Taxes? $ _____

What Do You Estimate You Spend?   − $ _____

NET CASH FLOW $ _____

STEP NINE: NET WORTH

Assets

Total Cash $ _____

Total Fixed Income $ _____

Total Stocks $ _____

Total Mutual Funds $ _____

Total Annuities $ _____

Total Other Assets $ _____

Total Retirement Accounts $ _____

Total Real Estate $ _____

TOTAL ASSETS $ _____

Liabilities

Total Credit-Card Debt $ _____

Total Student Loans $ _____

Total Personal Loans $ _____

Total Car/Boat Loans $ _____

Total Mortgages $ _____

Total All Other Debt $ _____

TOTAL LIABILITIES $ _____

Net Worth

Total Assets $ _____

− Total Liabilities − $ _____

ESTIMATED NET WORTH $ _____

GOAL FOR NET WORTH IN:

THREE YEARS _____ **FIVE YEARS** _____ **TEN YEARS** _____

Signed: _____ Date Completed: _____

Signed: _____

THE FINISHRICH ADVISOR QUESTIONNAIRE™

5 Questions to Ask Yourself, and 10 Questions to Ask the Advisor

My FinishRich Book Series™ (*Smart Women Finish Rich, Smart Couples Finish Rich,* and *The Finish Rich Workbook*) is designed to give you the tools it takes to live and finish rich. But even though you now have these tools, you may feel more comfortable hiring a financial coach to help you along the way. There is a lot to be said for doing this. Whether your aim is to buy a home, plan your retirement, or pay for a loved one's college education, working with an experienced professional financial advisor who truly supports and coaches you can make a huge difference in the speed and efficiency with which you achieve your financial goals and dreams.

So how do you find the perfect advisor? To begin with, it's critical that you prepare for the interview process. The **FinishRich Advisor Questionnaire™** is a handy form you can bring with you when you are interviewing potential advisors. Unless you're very lucky, you may need to interview numerous candidates before you find the one advisor who feels like the right fit. By using this questionnaire—along with the **FinishRich Advisor GradeCard™** that follows— you'll be able to decide with confidence on an advisor who meets your needs and qualifications.

But before you head off for your interview, you should know some things about yourself and what you want out of the relationship, and you should know what sort of answers you'll be looking for in the interview. So before you begin, here are five questions to ask yourself, followed by a discussion of each of the 10 questions you'll be asking your potential advisor.

5 QUESTIONS TO ASK YOURSELF

1. **Why do you want to hire a financial advisor?**

What are you looking to achieve with a financial advisor? Before you hire someone, make sure you really understand why you are doing this. What do you really want your money to help you do? What's really important to you? How do you see an advisor helping you achieve your values, dreams, and goals?

2. **What type of client are you?**

There are basically three types of clients: delegators, collaborators, and instigators. Knowing which type you are makes it easier to select the right advisor. Make sure you share with potential advisors what type of client you think you are. It will help them determine if they are suited to work with you.

▼ **Delegators** look for a professional to handle all the details. While they like to be updated on a regular basis, they are not interested in the minute details. They don't really want to follow the markets or their accounts on a daily basis. What they really want is a professional who will handle their money and guide them on making the decisions.

▼ **Collaborators** enjoy watching the markets and regularly read and study what is happening in the economy. They want to be involved in both the design and the monitoring of their portfolio and they regard a financial advisor as a member of their team. In short, they want to be involved but they also want advice.

▼ **Instigators** consider themselves to be financial experts. They are very knowledgeable and experienced about investing. They are not really looking for a great deal of advice but rather a professional off whom they can bounce their ideas and through whom they can place their trades and investment requests.

3. **How do you want to pay your advisor?**

Do you want to pay upfront (commissions), pay as you go (fee-based), or simply pay by the hour (fee-only). Everyone feels differently. Ultimately, professional advice is not free and you will have to pay something. The real question is what are you willing to pay a year for advice and how do you want to pay for it?

4. **What is your risk tolerance?**

Can you emotionally handle losing money? Be honest with yourself. Ask yourself right now how you would feel if you invested $10,000 and in less than a year it dropped in value to $8,000. What if you invested $10,000 and it grew to $12,000? Would you be more excited by growing your money by $2,000 in a year or more upset by losing that much? Share with your advisor how this experience would make you feel and how you think you would react.

5. **Are you really committed to your financial goals?**

A good financial advisor is a coach. But even the best coach can't help a player who isn't committed. No one can hope to achieve serious financial goals and dreams without equally serious commitment. Financial advisors are not miracle workers. In order to get anywhere, you need to save and invest and spend less than you earn—year in and year out. Are you committed to doing that? If you are, then a good financial advisor should be able to help you get where you want to go faster than doing it yourself.

10 QUESTIONS TO ASK A FINANCIAL ADVISOR

1. **How long have you been a financial advisor?**

This a very simple question—and yet almost no one ever asks it! Ask potential advisors how long they have been in the business and how long they have worked at their firm. If they previously worked at another financial firm, ask them why they moved.

2. **What makes you a good financial advisor?**

Start with this "warm-up" question before you ask for an advisor's specific qualifications. Let them tell you in their own words why they think they are a good financial advisor. Listen carefully to what they say and how they appear when they say it.

3. **What licenses, credentials, and other certifications do you have?**

Earlier, I suggested you go to **www.nasdr.com** to check out a potential advisor's credentials. But you should also ask potential advisors yourself to tell you what licenses and other certifications they have. If they tell you they are a "financial planner," ask them if they have a CFP (Certified Financial Planner) certification. If they tell you they do, double check by visiting **www.cfp.com**. Also, don't forget to ask candidates about their educational backgrounds.

Licenses they may or may not have include Securities, Insurance, Commodities, Registered Investment Advisor, Certified Financial Planner™ (CFP), Certified Public Accountant (CPA).

4. **Have you ever been disciplined by the NASD or any regulatory agency during your career?**

While relatively few advisors have ever been formally disciplined, I suggest you double-check what a potential advisor tells you in answer to this question. You can do this by visiting www.nasdr.com. There you can input the advisor's name and firm, and find out if either he or she has any "disclosure events" on their records. If they do, it could mean your potential advisor has had past legal problems, and you can request additional details online.

4. **What type of clients do you specialize in?**

Some advisors specialize in a very specific niche. They may focus their entire practice around doctors, corporate retirees, women divorcees, business owners. If the advisor is more of a generalist, then ask him or her to describe a typical client to you (age, assets, job, etc.).

5. **What services do you and your firm offer?**

Most financial firms today offer a wide array of financial planning products and services. Ask the advisor to share with you (in writing if possible) just what those products and services include. An advisor should be able to provide you with a brochure or information packet that explains in detail all the different things his or her firm can do for you. Planning services might include financial planning, retirement planning, insurance planning, estate planning, and taxes. Products might include stocks, mutual funds, bonds, options, managed money accounts, annuities, commodities, hedge funds, or others.

6. **Do you create a written financial plan for your clients?**

Some advisors provide extremely detailed plans and others provide nothing. Ask the advisor specifically what type of plan he or she prepares for clients. Is there a cost for this planning and its process? Can you show me a sample of the kind of plan you use with your clients?

7. **Do you spend time educating your clients about money?**

How an advisor answers this question should help you determine if this is an advisor who wants you to be an educated investor or rather simply wants you to turn over your finances to them and not ask questions. Many advisors offer investment classes, books, tapes, brochures, and educational videos—all designed to help their clients become smarter about money.

8. **How do you service your clients?**

Ask the advisor how exactly his or her firm takes care of its clients. Ask if the firm has a team in place to handle the workload—and if so, how many people are on the team? Who creates the financial plan? Who handles the transfer of my money? Who watches how my investments are doing? Who will call me to schedule review meetings and be my general contact?

9. **How do you charge your clients?**

This is one of the most important questions you need to get answered, for it will tell you a lot about what type of advisor you are dealing with. As noted earlier, there are basically four ways advisors are paid:

▼ **Commission.** Every time the advisor buys or sells an investment for you, he receives a commission on the transaction. Commissions can range from as little as .025% to as much as 5.5% of the total investment, depending on the kind of product involved.

▼ **Fee-Based.** A fee-based financial advisor typically charges a yearly fee that is determined by the amount of assets they are managing for you. These fees generally range from .050% to 3%. The more they manage, the lower the percentage they charge.

▼ **Fee-Only.** A fee-only advisor charges by the hour for their time and advice. Always ask this type of planner if he or she receives any other compensation for recommending particular investments. An advisor who gets commissions based on your investment selections is not a true fee-only advisor.

▼ **Combination Fee and Commission.** Some planners do a combination of charging for a financial plan and then offering either a commission-based relationship or a fee-based relationship. Make sure you get your advisor to put in writing what he or she charges so that you know precisely what it's going to cost you before you invest.

10. **How many clients do you have?**

Find out how many clients the advisor is currently working with. How much money are they currently managing and what is the size of a typical account? Where will you fall in terms of client size? Will you be one of their bigger accounts, or one of the smaller ones? Many advisors maintain a ranking system for clients. Does your advisor do this? If so, ask how they rank their clients and where you would rank among them.

Now you're ready to go to your first appointment, with **The FinishRich Advisor Questionnaire** in hand.

THE FINISHRICH ADVISOR QUESTIONNAIRE™

1. Advisor Information

First appointment scheduled for: _____

Name of advisor: _____

Firm: _____

Address: _____

_____

Phone: _____

Fax: _____

E-mail: _____

2. How long have you been a financial advisor?

Years in the business: _____

Years at their firm: _____

Why he or she switched firms:

3. What makes you a good financial advisor?

The answer in advisor's own words:

Your notes on the advisor's demeanor:

4. What is your educational background and what licenses, credentials, and other certifications do you have?

Education

Undergraduate Degree	❑	In _____	From what university? _____
Advanced Degree	❑	In _____	From what university? _____
Master's Degree	❑	In _____	From what university? _____

Licenses

Securities ❑

Insurance ❑

Commodities ❑

Registered Investment Advisor ❑

Certified Financial Planner™ (CFP) ❑

Certified Public Accountant (CPA) ❑

5. Have you ever been disciplined by the NASD or any regulatory agency during your career?

Advisor's answer:

Did what he say jibe with what you found by checking the records at www.nasdr.com?

6. What type of clients do you specialize in?

Advisor's niche: _____

If your advisor has no niche, then ask:
Could you please describe a typical client?

Age of typical client: _____

Size of assets of typical client: _____

Occupation of typical client: _____

7. What services do you and your firm offer?

Check ones that apply:

Planning services		Example of products	
Financial planning	❏	Stocks	❏
Retirement planning	❏	Mutual funds	❏
Insurance planning	❏	Bonds	❏
Estate planning	❏	Options	❏
Taxes	❏	Managed money	❏
		Annuities	❏
		Commodities	❏
		Hedge funds	❏
		Other _____	

Advisor gave you a brochure or information packet to take home   Yes ❏   No ❏

8. Do you create a written financial plan for your clients?

Yes ❏   No ❏

If yes, ask:

What sort of plan?

Cost, if any, for the plan or the time spent preparing it:

Advisor gave you a sample plan to peruse   Yes ❏   No ❏

7. Do you spend time educating your clients about money?

Yes ❏   No ❏

If yes, then how?

Classes ❏
Books ❏
Tapes ❏
Brochures ❏
Educational videos ❏

8. Who will be involved in my service?

The Financial Plan: Who creates the plan?

Name: _____ Phone _____ E-mail_____

The Transfer: Who handles the transfer of my money?

Name: _____ Phone _____ E-mail_____

The Monitor: Who watches how my investments are doing?

Name: _____ Phone _____ E-mail_____

The Service: Who calls me to schedule review meetings?

Name: _____ Phone _____ E-mail_____

9. How do you charge your clients?

Commission   ❏
If so, what is the range of commissions?

Fee-Based   ❏
If so, what is the annual fee scale?

Fee-Only   ❏
If so, what is your hourly rate? How are the hours calculated?

Does the advisor receive any other compensation for recommending particular investments?

Combination Fee & Commission   ❏
Provide details:

Will the advisor put the fee arrangement in writing?   Yes ❏   No ❏

10. How many clients do you have?

Number of clients: _____

Total assets under management: $_____

Your rank among them in terms of size of assets: _____

	BEST	A	B	C	D	F	WORST
	THE FINISHRICH ADVISOR GRADECARD™						
REFERRAL	I received a referral from a CPA, attorney, or trusted friend who has worked with the advisor for years.						I walked in off the street to a brokerage firm or a bank and asked to speak with a financial advisor.
FIRST CONTACT	When I called the advisor for an appointment, I received a professional response indicating that the advisor had a set system for handling "first appointments."						It was not clear that the advisor had any kind of systematic "first appointment" process. He offered to come to my house.
FIRST GREETING	When I arrived at the advisor's office, I was greeted quickly and professionally. The advisor was expecting me and had a file with my name on it prepared for the meeting.						I was kept waiting for my appointment or otherwise greeted unprofessionally. The advisor did not have a file ready for our meeting.
THE FINISHRICH INVENTORY PLANNER™	The advisor provided me with a form similar to the FinishRich Inventory Planner that requested I bring a list of financial documents to our first meeting, including my tax returns and 401(k) statements.						The advisor didn't ask me to bring anything to our first meeting.
FIRST IMPRESSION	The advisor's office was neat and well-organized. There were no other clients' files in open view on the advisor's desk.						The advisor's office was a mess. Files, research reports, and newspapers cluttered the desk. I could see files containing other clients' private information.
FIRST APPOINTMENT	The advisor asked probing, pertinent questions during our first meeting. She took the time to get to know me and really seemed to take an interest in my goals, values, dreams, and family situation.						The advisor immediately started "selling me" on investment products, her firm's reputation, and her credentials.

THE FINISHRICH ADVISOR GRADECARD™							
	BEST	A	B	C	D	F	WORST
ADVISOR EXPERIENCE	The advisor has a great deal of experience. She has been in the business for more than five years, manages more than $50 million in assets, and appears to have many satisfied clients.						The advisor just finished her training and is brand new to the business. She has less than $10 million under management.
ADVISOR PHILOSOPHY	The advisor explained in detail his investment philosophy. He has a clear system for managing money that I understand and feel comfortable with.						The advisor was confusing. Most of what he said went over my head. I'm not really clear what his investment philosophy is for managing money.
FINANCIAL PLAN	The advisor prepared a written financial plan that I find clear and easy to understand. I learned a great deal by going through the planning process.						The advisor did not prepare a written plan. Or if he did, I really don't understand it.
FEES	The advisor fully explained the nature of all the fees associated with working with him. I received a copy of the fee structure in writing and I understand it.						The advisor did not explain how he gets paid.
THE CLOSE	The advisor did not pressure me to make a decision about whether I wanted to work with him. He was courteous at all times, respectful of my questions, and easygoing.						The advisor tried to pressure me to make a decision. He insisted that time is of the essence and I need to act now.
MY GUT FEELING	My gut tells me that this financial advisor is qualified to coach me, will put my best interests first, and is someone I can trust.						Something doesn't feel right. I can't put my finger on it, but I'm not entirely comfortable with this advisor.

About the Author

David Bach is the author of the national bestsellers *Smart Women Finish Rich* and *Smart Couples Finish Rich.* The host of his own PBS special, "Smart Women Finish Rich," Bach is an internationally recognized financial advisor, author, and educator.

Bach is the creator of the FinishRich Book and Seminar Series™, which has allowed millions of people to benefit from his quick and easy-to-use financial strategies. In just the last few years, over 300,000 people have attended his Smart Women Finish Rich™ and Smart Couples Finish Rich™ Seminars, which have been taught throughout North America in over 1,500 cities. Each month, through these seminars, men and women learn firsthand how to take smart financial action to live a life in line with their values.

Regularly featured on television and radio, as well as in newspapers and magazines, Bach has appeared on ABC's *The View,* NBC's *Weekend Today,* CBS's *The Early Show,* Fox News Channel's *The O'Reilly Factor,* CNN, CNBC, and MSNBC, and he has been profiled in major publications, including *BusinessWeek, USA Today, People,* the *Financial Times,* the *Washington Post, The Wall Street Journal,* the *Los Angeles Times,* the *San Francisco Chronicle, Working Women,* and *Family Circle.* Bestseller lists that have featured *Smart Women Finish Rich* include the *New York Times* and *Wall Street Journal* business lists, *BusinessWeek,* the *Washington Post,* the *Boston Globe,* and the *San Francisco Chronicle. Smart Couples Finish Rich* has also appeared on the *New York Times* business, *BusinessWeek, USA Today, Denver Post,* and *San Francisco Chronicle* bestseller lists. His books are currently printed in five languages.

A renowned financial speaker, Bach presents seminars and keynotes each year to the world's leading financial-services firms, Fortune 500 companies, universities, and national conferences. Today, Bach is the CEO of FinishRich™ Inc., a company dedicated to revolutionizing the way people learn about money. Prior to founding FinishRich™ Inc., Bach was the senior president of a major New York brokerage firm and a partner of The Bach Group (1993 to 2001), which managed over a half billion dollars for individual investors during his tenure.

David Bach is a contributing editor to *Smart Money* magazine. He lives in New York with his wife, Michelle. Please visit his Web site at www.finishrich.com.

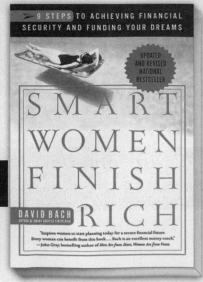

Attend a FinishRich™ Seminar

My grandmother taught me anyone could be rich if they had the right tools and the right motivation. Now I want to teach you! Come to a Smart Women Finish Rich™ or Smart Couples Finish Rich™ Seminar—or both!

They have been taught to thousands of people who have learned—just as you can—that improving their financial lives can be easy and fun. You will also learn how to focus on your values so that the money you do spend enhances the life you always dreamed of living.

Both seminars are usually offered at no cost and include a free workbook.

To see David live or attend a FinishRich™ Seminar in your area, please visit:

www.finishrich.com

How to Reach Us

. . . go to finishrich.com

If you would like more information about the FinishRich Book Series™, FinishRich Seminars™, and other financial education tools and services we offer, please contact us at www.finishrich.com. There you will find the following information:

- My free online FinishRich™ newsletter
- How to attend a Smart Couples Finish Rich and/or Smart Women Finish Rich Seminar™
- How to hire David Bach or one of his FinishRich speakers to speak at your next event
- Books and book updates
- Audiotapes
- Videos
- Interactive CD-rom
- For financial advisors only: How to become licensed to teach FinishRich Seminars™
- Coming soon . . . information on my next two books, *The Automatic Millionaire* (expected release October 2003) and *Start Young, Finish Rich* (expected release 2004)

To everyone who has written and e-mailed me . . . THANK YOU from the bottom of my heart. I am incredibly grateful and humbled by the letters and e-mails we continue to receive on a daily basis. If this book has made an impact on you, please know that I love to hear from my readers. You are the reason I do what I do. If you send an e-mail with your success stories, ideas, suggestions, and/or questions to success@finishrich.com, I promise I will read it. Maybe your personal story (if you give us permission) will become part of a future book.

Lastly, I'm about to start work on *Start Young, Finish Rich* and we are actively looking for young people to share their experiences with money, both good and bad. If you are under the age of 30, or know someone who is, and would like to be a part of our next book, please visit our Web site for details. We would love for you to join us on this journey to live and finish rich!

—David Bach